I0213886

TWIXT MYTH AND HISTORY

Also by Robert Barclay

Non-fiction

The Art of the Trumpet-maker
The Preservation and Use of Historic Musical Instruments
Making a Natural Trumpet (with M. Münkwitz and R. Seraphinoff)
Henry VIII's Motorcycle: Or a Tale of Two Trumpets

Fiction

Triple Take: A Museum Story
Death at the Podium
Ask Me About My Bombshells
Jacob the Trumpeter
His Majesty's Grand Conceit
Conversations Between Sensible People

Cover art: Loose Cannon Designs
Image by Freepik

TWIXT MYTH AND HISTORY

TWENTY-FIVE INTERVIEWS ACROSS THE AGES

hosted by

Robert Barclay

LIBRARY AND ARCHIVES CANADA CATALOGUING IN PUBLICATION

Title: Twixt myth and history : twenty-five interviews across the ages / as hosted by Robert Barclay.
Names: Barclay, R. L., author
Identifiers: Canadiana 20240536819 | ISBN 9781988657387 (softcover)
Subjects: LCSH: Imaginary interviews. | LCSH: Celebrities. | LCSH: Mythology. | LCGFT: Interviews. | LCGFT: Fiction.
Classification: LCC PS8603.A7244 T85 2025 | DDC C818/.607 – dc23

Published by
LOOSE CANNON PRESS

www.loosecannonpress.com

Contents

Credits

The idea for this book came from a discussion about what Jesus Christ would have to say if he was invited to sit down at a table in Starbucks. My writing colleagues Alex Binkley, Katherine Williams, Elisabeth Russ, Brenda Fedun, and Ken Byers would gather at Ten Toes coffee house in Ottawa every Tuesday afternoon. A year or so ago they invited me to join them at their Toesday meetings, and here is the result of their literary stimulation. Jon Peirce gave me valuable advice during the compilation and preparation of the text, Lena Samson cast her eagle eye over the proofs, and several family members and friends were afflicted with texts in various states of repair. Thanks everybody for your input into the creation of this absurd volume.

Bob Barclay
Ottawa, 2025

Overture

We are always doing something for posterity, but I would fain see posterity do something for us
Joseph Addison

Many characters from history, legend, folklore, and myth have been given a bad ride by posterity. Some of these figures are in part imaginary anyway, but if even they do have a toehold in history, Clio herself tries to shut the door on it. And because the lives of these figures are not well documented, incidents, actions, and just plain fabrications gather around them. The Muse of History throws a profound reporting bias at them. The fundamental human compulsion to mythologize is to blame, of course. But deep in the tissues, webs, skeins, and ramifications of these figures' collected narratives lie kernels of truth, and that's what I'm after.

I am what H.G. Wells described as a chronic argonaut, having the dubious fortune of slipping my anchor from the here and now. This means I am able to meet these characters one-on-one, either in my own spatio/temporal location or in theirs. I can choose the time and place of our meetings, sometimes visiting them in their milieu and sometimes inviting them to visit me.

I must say, to a large extent I have found these characters obliging and not in the least reticent in sharing their particular viewpoints once the strange circumstances have been explained to them. It's a catharsis for them. There has been occasional antagonism, but this is brought about by jarring disparities between our modern readings and hitherto unanticipated verities. In other words, over time and retelling, truths have been suppressed and untruths have been promulgated, and nobody appreciates history telling lies about them. Sometimes, through no fault of mine, I have got the wrong end of the stick. Only one of these interviews ended badly (how was I to know Sir Richard Whittington would be so thin skinned?) and I consider this an excellent record. To a greater extent, my interviews have helped straighten their stories out, for which I am sure they were/are/will be grateful.

On reading these interviews, the linguistic advantages of transtemporal cultural placement will be immediately apparent. Simply put, I speak their language when I travel to them, and they speak mine when they come to me. It hasn't been easy rendering these conversations comprehensible to modern readers. I've done my best by all of them, and even though I have put language into their mouths, I am certain they would neither complain nor criticize. Hard to see how they could do either really.

With Godgyfa in Coventry

It's nice you could find time for me. Not that you really have an option. Here, have a chocolate.'

'Chocolate? What is this?'

'Try one.'

'Why's there a picture of a naked woman on horseback on the box?'

'It's based on your legend. An accolade.'

'*My* legend? What legend? Who are you, and why am I here?'

'Here, try this one. It's filled with a creamy white chocolate ganache laced with vanilla, and encased in a dark chocolate shell.'

'But it's got a naked woman on horseback pressed into it! Come on, what *is* this all about?'

'Try it. I think you'll appreciate our 21st century Belgian chocolate science.'

... It's delicious, but why haven't you answered my question? Give me another... No, not a naked woman this time! I'll take the one with the lion rampant. Thanks. So, what's this all about?'

'Well, I have this God-given—no pun intended—gift of time-sliding, a kind of chrono-tourism. I can either go back or I can bring folks forward. I thought you'd approve of the latter, so you could see how your legend has progressed from the vantage point of a chocolatier in Coventry.'

'What legend? I don't know what you're talking about. I just told you.'

'You mean, no Lady Godiva's naked horse ride through the streets of Coventry? That *is* disappointing.'

'Naked ride!? Are you insane? Send me back, right now!'

'No, no, please bear with me. I'm clearly not acquainted with your full story.'

'Obviously. So, just tell me what you think you know.'

'Well, your husband Leofric, Earl of Mercia and Lord of Coventry, was imposing considerable taxes upon his subjects.'

'So? We founded a Benedictine house together, St Osburg's, in… what would that be… 1043? The Danes razed the nunnery in 1016. It's an expensive business, running a monastery: abbot, monks, building, furnishings, upkeep. Somebody has to pay.'

'And the charter assigned the income of 24 villages in the precinct of Coventry to Leofric for maintenance of the house.'

'You know more than you let on. True, and I endowed the monastery myself, gave gold and silver from my trinkets and baubles, and I had Wustan the silversmith make some votive pieces from the metal. Nice play on my name, by the way: *Godgyfa*, gift *of* God, but *Godgyfu*, gift *to* God. Not bad, eh?'

'I'm no judge, but let's get to the bareback riding. You see, according to the legend, you argued with Leofric that the taxes were too high, and that the good people of Coventry were suffering, but he refused to budge.'

'Oh, yes, I remember I did argue with the old skinflint but he was adamant. See, people—ordinary people—couldn't come anywhere near him to complain, while I heard all sorts of gripes from the town and surrounds through my ladies. I really did fear that he would have a kind of rebellion on his hands, but he was as tight as a fish's arsehole with money.'

'Hence his reputed gambit?'

'Which was?'

'He stated that he would only ease the tax burden on the peasants if you were to ride naked on horseback through the centre of Coventry.'

'*Good God Almighty!* Totally taken out of context! Yes, he did say that, but he was *joking!* I even remember what the old bastard said: "Oh, sure, the day I ease the peasants' burden is the day you ride your horse tit-naked through the streets of Coventry!" He didn't even know what I looked like naked. Only my ladies did.'

'So, a simple joke between two people?'

'Of course. And you tell me, over a thousand years later that's what's on these chocolates! You *are* insane!'

'So, you swear this didn't happen?'

'*Didn't happen?* May I leave the truth of that to your prurient imagination? And stop looking me over like that!'

'Sorry. Well, the story is that your compassion and heartfelt concern for the good people of Coventry overcame your… er… reluctance, but you did command that the people remain indoors with their windows and doors barred, and not to peep. One fellow peeped but he was struck blind. Chap by the name of Tom.'

'*Who?* Who would spread this *infamy?*'

'And your hair was so long that when you let it down it covered your… covered… er, like a cloak.'

'Who, I asked? Who would spread this infamy?'

'I don't know, because I cannot fathom how a jest between two people in private could spawn a legend.'

'Well, it did, didn't it? Maybe one of my ladies…? They're such tattling bitches, but even so…'

'The story first appears in the early 13th century in *Flores Historiarum* by Roger of Wendover, but he took stuff without any judgement from much earlier works.'

'I want to pin it down! I want to pin the culprit down and tear his balls from his living loins!'

'Sadly, there is never one single perpetrator. History is a progressive series of tales, some of which are true, and some of which are false, while the majority lie somewhere in between. Your legend, I fear, is one of those that had a slight element of truth and moved through the ages into eminently believable falsehood.'

'Why? Why would anyone so impugn my virtue?'

'As I explained, no single person did. I wouldn't be at all surprised if some future generations latched onto the germ of your story and used it as a lesson in humility: "Such was her devotion to her people that she would bare all for them", that sort of thing. Or perhaps a sexually repressed society, like the Puritans or Evangelists, used the very idea of publicly exposed naked womanhood as an indictment upon immodesty. After all, they're the horniest of all in secret, the sexually repressed ones.'

'What *are* you talking about?'

'Oh, nothing. Nothing at all. Here, have another chocolate. The rampant lion is the one with the buttery salted caramel centre encased in dark chocolate.'

'What in hell is buttery salted caramel?'

In 1926, Pierre Draps Sr began making pralines in his home workshop in Brussels. He was deeply inspired by the legend of Lady Godiva and named the company in her honour. Values associated with Lady Godiva such as boldness, standing up for what is right, and a pioneering spirit still inform GODIVA's ethos today. And their chocolates are excellent.

A Barbecue with Attila

Here, pull up a chair at this picnic table. You can park your Harley over there on the grass. I'm so glad you accepted my barbecue invitation Mr… er… Hun…'

'No, really, call me Attila. Everybody does. Or rampaging, pillaging, murdering bastard sometimes. Attila's quicker.'

'I like the leathers and studs and chains. Fits your image somehow.'

'Well, dropping down here from the Big Upstairs I figured I should look the part. Swap a horse for a hog and there you go.'

'And the tattoos and shaved head complete the image.'

'Yeah, swarthy, that's me. Hey, these ribs are fantastic. What sauce do they use?'

'I wouldn't be surprised if it's a secret recipe, but oranges, tomatoes, and tamarinds have to figure in it somewhere.'

'Don't know what the fuck any of that stuff is, but it tastes great!'

'Glad you like it. Here, let me pour you a beer. Now, tell me Mr… er, Attila. I guess from beyond the grave you've heard the somewhat derogatory epithets that have been attached to your name.'

'What like "rampaging, pillaging, murdering bastard" you mean?'

'Something like that.'

'What about the Romans, then? Think they didn't go around rampaging and pillaging and murdering? Made us look like friggin' amateurs, they did.'

'So, the epithets and the legend are unjustified?'

'Shit, yes! Let me tell you it's all… Yeshua, these ribs are damned good! Gimme some more, will you? Love to crunch those bones.'

'It's all what? You were saying…'

'Eh? Oh, yeah. It's all stuff my enemies made up. See, they wrote things down.'

'And you didn't.'

'Look, everybody knows that Huns, Alans, Ostrogoths,

Gepids, the whole crowd didn't even know what writing was. What's the word for that?'

'Illiterate?'

'Yeah, that's it; illiterate. See, you don't get to be king of a vast, mobile horde of vassal tribes and rampage over half of the Roman Empire if your nose is stuck in books. Wow, this beer! Never drunk anything like it! What kind is it?'

'It's from a local microbrewery. A nice hoppy IPA.'

'And an illiterate rampaging, pillaging, murdering bastard is supposed to know what the fuck you're talking about? Greek to me. Or Latin.'

'IPA means Indi... oh, forget it. Anyhow, you say your bad rap is due to biased reporting then?'

'Course it is! Look at the shit storm over Honoria.'

'What do you say happened?'

'What do you mean "what do *you* say"? You fucking with me?'

'All right, all right, *your* perspective...'

'Okay, I was on real buddy-buddy terms with Emperor Valentinian III, but his sister Honoria wrote to me saying some Roman senator was trying to get his leg over her, so how about we get married instead?'

'Yes, but the story I read was that you interpreted her letter as a marriage proposal.'

'Interpreted my ass! She sent her goddamned engagement ring with the letter, for Jeshua's sake! When I had it read to me, what was I supposed to think?'

'So, you accepted her proposal of marriage at face value?'

'Damn right I did. You ever seen her? The mosaics don't do her justice. Gimme some more beer, this is thirsty work. And some more of those ribs.'

'I heard that Valentinian didn't believe a word of it, and was all set to kill his sister.'

'He was really pissed! I think her mum prevented him from offing her, but she got kicked out of court anyway. Damned if I know where she went.'

'Of course, she had been a thorn in Valentinian's side for many years, hadn't she? Even so, you thought it was a disproportionate reaction?'

'Well, she'd been putting out for years; anyone in a toga who could stand to attention. See, she was kind of uppity, know what I mean? Thought women should have some sort of say in decisions, politics, things like that. Dangerous, but oh so appealing! But, yeah, Valentinian's reaction was over the top.'

'Well, you did send one of your emissaries to Ravenna to demand half of the Western Empire as dowry, and to threaten an immediate invasion if you were turned down.'

'Yeah, I did do that... But listen: her giving half of it away, me taking it by force, or the whole thing folding up anyway. It's debatable.'

'But the invasion is a fact?'

'Oh, sure. Flushed all my vassals out of the woodwork: Gepids, Ostrogoths, Rugians, Scirians, Heruls, Thuringians, Alans, Burgundians... shit, you name it, they all joined the march to Belgica! Must have been half a million of us.'

'And you sacked Metz and Strasbourg and many other towns.'

'Aw, c'mon, you're parroting the written stuff again. We were *liberating* these places from the Romans and Christians and such. A mission of mercy. But in the end the Romans and Visigoths ganged up on us...'

'Actually, they forced you back east and thrashed you at Catalaunum.'

'Brief setback, man. You've been reading the wrong stuff. You brought me down here to straighten things out, right?'

'Yes, of course, your version.'

'*The* version! We left Catalaunum in our own good time. Thrashing my ass! And I came back in fine style, did I not, liberating a whole slew of Italian cities. You visited Venice?'

'Sure, it's a modern-day tourist magnet. Why?'

'All mine! The buggers were so scared of being liberated

they ran out into the sea and built houses on stilts out in the lagoon. That's Venice. Thank you, thank you, you're very welcome!'

'I read that your army razed Aquileia so completely that it was hard to find the original site.'

'There you go again! That garbage was written centuries after the event from hearsay by some old bastard who hadn't a clue. Classic example of libeling someone who can't fight back because he's dead.'

'But in the end, you had to sign a peace treaty. That's a piece of historical fact.'

'Oh, sure. That bastard Valentinian sent the Pope and some other guys up to Mincio with pens and parchment. We would've withdrawn anyway as we were starving and diseased and out of weapons, but they didn't know that. Didn't let on, of course.'

'Apparently, Pope Leo warned you that, should you sack Rome, God would visit the same fate on you as on Alaric.'

'Bullshit! Christian fearmongering. As if I'd fall for that divine justice horseshit. We quit because there was no chance of winning. End of story and no fucking regrets. Never did get into Honoria's stola, though…'

'So, in summary, we could say… sorry, would you mind not crunching those bones and belching for just a moment? Thank you… we could say that history favours the literate.'

'Damn right! Goddamned outrage how my honest intentions have been treated.'

'So, finally, what would be your message to posterity?'

'Listen, you kids everywhere: take some advice from old Uncle Attila. If you want history to judge you well, and you're a rampaging, pillaging, murdering bastard, make sure you learn your ABCs. Then you can write it all down the way it should be, and you'll all be national heroes like Napoleon Buonaparte, instead of rampaging, pillaging, murdering bastards.'

A Café at the Vieux-Marché in Rouen

What in hell can I tell you that hasn't been written already? Look, from my perfect perspective, up there where the saints dwell, I can see it all across the centuries. I am one of the most written-about and celebrated saints or sinners anywhere in the Western world, so make it brief.'

'I brought you to the Vieux-Marché here in Rouen to perhaps... focus our discussion.'

'Thank you very much for that, you insensitive bastard. Can almost smell the smoke.'

'Well, I thought you might like to see how the centuries have revered the place of your martyrdom.'

'*Revered?* Totally incomprehensible; blue jeans, traffic, cafés, chewing gum, pigeon shit. And that cross is just plain weird. Do they think I was crucified, or what?'

'Well... the cross... Christian identity...'

'Yeah, yeah, I get it. I suppose it'd be difficult to have a monument made out of faggots of wood.'

'Quite. The thing is, in this age we are very focused on gender and identity and feminism, and you are regarded as a blazing beacon of fem...'

'*Fuck you!*'

'Oh, I am *so* sorry... That was careless. I didn't mean...'

'Not getting off to a very good start, are we? Want to try making another first impression?'

'Let me rephrase that...'

'No, no. I know what you're getting at: a little girl in plate armour and chainmail kicking ass among the big, important men. How *did* she do it?'

'Yes, I suppose that is the gist of it. You were just a small girl from a peasant family in northern France. So, what happened?'

'You really wanna know? Well, when I was about 13 or 14 Burgundian troops attacked our village, Domrémy, looting and plundering. The villagers all knew the Armagnacs were the rightful rulers of France, and that's when the Archangel Michael appeared to me and told me to support

Charles the Dauphin and help kick the English backside out of France.'

'What a vision! But a young maiden in a small village. That's a pretty grandiose aspiration.'

'Well, first of all, you'd tell me I was massively schizophrenic. In your world it's treated like an illness; you people try to knock it down with chemicals. When I lived you could play it into something. It helped that there was this story going the rounds; a prophesy that an armed virgin with a banner would emerge to save France. I knew that was me, and so did everybody else.'

'But how did you manage to get recognized?'

'Powerful female wiles, my friend. I was a *presence*. Mind you, it took about three years before I was taken seriously. I went to Vaucouleurs with my uncle and petitioned Robert de Baudricort, but he wasn't buying. It took three tries before he'd listen, but Michael, and Saint Margaret and Saint Catherine as well, urged me on. (They were real, you know.) Then Baudricort sent me to see the Dauphin Charles VI in Chinon. I was now wearing men's clothing fulltime, and I looked very fine in doublet, tunic and cap, with my hair cut short. Bit of cross-dressing got him all in a tizzy, specially when I prophesied that he would be the next King of France.'

'And at that point your fame was spreading, was it not?'

'For sure. By this time, a virgin clad in chainmail with a breastplate and helmet could turn any man's head. I was the epitome of the prophesy. I tell you, these big, bold, clever men don't ever realize their dicks are making all the decisions. Charles was convinced of my purity and dedication, so off I went to relieve the siege of Orléans at the head of an army with my banner flying, sword in hand. Gullible fool.'

'But it worked. Only nine days after you arrived the siege was lifted and the English fled.'

'Oh, yes! Grown men all heartened by a slender virgin. I was only 17 but I was a force to be reckoned with, and didn't

I just know it. We chased them up the Loire; town after town falling—Jargeau, Meung-sur-Loire, Beaugency—and then cleaned the floor with them at Patay.'

'Then there was the coronation.'

'In Reims. The Dauphin became Charles VII, and I stood beside him. Man, that was the pinnacle! You know we French eventually wiped the English off our boots, and left them with nothing but Calais? It all started with me. But you know what, now I had done what Saint Michael told me I should do, he abandoned me…'

'Abandoned…?'

'Yes. Him, Saint Margaret, Saint Catherine, all of them. They never came again.'

'But you described your visions in great detail to the inquisitors at your trial.'

'So, I lied. They'd long since gone. By the time they had me on the stand I would've sworn that holy water was piss.'

'The visions had gone because the prophesy had been fulfilled?'

'I dunno. That's what I believe now, because I've had 600 years to think about it. I mean, you can't just get cured of schizophrenia, can you? It's with you for life. It won't just go away. No, those visions were real. Anyhow, at that time I was still full of piss and vinegar. I had Paris in my sights, still held by the English and the hated Burgundians. So, I marched with Charles VII and his whole goddamned army and we camped at La Chapelle. But when I prayed in the chapel of Sainte Geneviève before the assault, I knew it; that's the point when things started to come apart. Not a God-damned peep from my prayers; nothing. Abandoned.'

'And that was also where your image was becoming tarnished in the eyes of the nobility.'

'Oh, thank you very much! Why don't you just rub it in? Yes, the siege of Paris was a total cock up. I was dragged away from the siege with a hole in my thigh from a crossbow bolt, and that swine Charles refused to let me back into the fight.

Of course, without me the whole thing fell to pieces. Probably would have anyway.'

'So, you wanted to rejoin the siege even though you were injured?'

'Look, I got an arrow in my shoulder at Les Tourelles, I got a mighty headache when my helmet was split by a rock in Jargeau, and lots of smaller injuries besides. When you're on a mission you're immortal. Of course, after Paris... It's a grievous sin to contemplate taking your own life, but you're allowed to leave it in the hands of others, aren't you?'

'Suicide by cop...'

'What?'

'Oh, just something we say.'

'Well, stop saying it.'

'Charles must still have had some faith in you because you attacked La Charité together.'

'Failure. It was pissing rain, we were ill-equipped—not enough artillery, not enough food—but more to the point, little cross-dressing virgins can't inspire anybody in a siege more than once. Doesn't work that way. Up front on a charger, banner waving, that's where your virgins rally the troops. What a mess!'

'Then you organized a company of volunteers for the relief of Compiègne.'

'Should have known better. Driven by reputation, not saints whispering in my ear. The Burgundian scum had besieged the town; we failed and I was taken prisoner. I tried to escape a couple of times, but in the end the bastards handed me over to the English.'

'And that's when you were put on trial for heresy.'

'Right. Once I was in English hands that was the end of me. Real men humiliated in battle by a little girl? That was a real cock shriveller right there. They would do anything to find me guilty. *Anything*. So, they threw me in a cell, watched over by men twenty-four/seven, as you would put it. Chained up, the whole bit.'

'When you were imprisoned, did they try to… I mean, were you… er, molested?'

'Oh, cut to the chase! If you mean raped, say so! No, I was not. As soon as you let on they might be copulating with a demon, you can watch them droop as they back off.'

'Erm… er… yes. You… you were tried by Bishop Pierre Cauchon.'

'Yes, the *cochon*, a Burgundian tool. He did everything he could to prove heresy. They didn't have anything in all their books about cross-dressing, so they had to invent that bit. Anyway, the visions and my refusal to cooperate did it for me anyway. Heresy beyond a shadow of doubt. Off to the pile of faggots, quick march.'

'In a reinvestigation in 1456, the trial was found to be tainted by deceit and procedural errors.'

'Oh, ye-e-es. I tell you, it's really gratifying to be judged innocent post mortem. Still, I did get an upgrade to Saint eventually, so that's nice. I should have a framed certificate on my wall, like in a doctor's office.'

'But you are celebrated throughout the world as an early feminist icon, a symbol of freedom and independence, and a patron saint of France. Your image is a force to this day.'

'It's amazing to me that in your day and age women still need boosting by someone like me to put the big, clever men in their place. Maybe more of your women should put on armour and chainmail, start swinging swords and lopping off a few cocks?'

'Yes, well… er… Thank you. It's been a revelation to me, speaking to you here and hearing your views firsthand.'

'Oh, yeah. Sitting at a sidewalk café, drinking this coffee muck, and reminiscing about the good old days. It's been a blast.'

A Chat in Cremona

Hello Signor Stradivari. It's good of you to find the time for a meeting. It's certainly a busy place with these dozens of craftsmen working away.'

'Come into the office, it's a little quieter there. Oh, excuse me please… Yes, what is it? No, we're not pushing the Paris batch ahead of Lisboa; I already told Roberto. Now… my apologies. Come this way. Put your suitcase in the corner.'

'I really am distracting you from your business…'

'No, really, it'll be a pleasure to shut myself away. It runs itself. Usually…'

'I had no idea this would be a factory. I had the impression of a sole craftsman working relatively alone.'

'Really? Whyever did you think that?'

'Well, your lifetime's work, well over a thousand instruments…'

'Get outa here! We've done ten times that many. Think we're sitting on our hands, or what?'

'I meant you personally.'

'Me personally? I haven't made a violin from start to finish since before I opened the factory. Couldn't have individuals doing that. We just don't work that way.'

'How do mean?'

'Piecework, of course. You saw the workshop outside; a man for every piece. We get orders from all over Europa; it's the only way to keep up.'

'And we had this idea of you working alone in splendid isolation, crafting each violin with meticulous attention. That's how we imagine you. Could I show you a picture?'

'A picture? Of me?'

'Oh, yes. Could you pass me my suitcase? Thanks… Here, this is how we see you, but just looking around the shop, I'm…'

'Oh, my good God almighty! *Hey Roberto, Guiseppe, come see this!* It's the great philosopher in deep contemplation. And look at those clothes! Just come back from a wedding, or maybe a funeral. And what about the mess! Nobody could work like that. Christ, I'd kill you guys if you scattered half-finished fiddles all over the shop. All right, stop laughing and get back to work. Oh… my… God!'

'I'm beginning to think that our image of you is somewhat... coloured.'

'Oh, is it *really?* Listen, the Stradivari shop has its fine reputation for two things: prompt attention to every customer, and rigorous inspection during building and again before they go out. I examine them white...'

'White?'

'All finished but before the varnish. And if the fiddle doesn't meet my high standards, it goes back to the bench for more work. And a roasting for whoever didn't meet my requirements. Then after the varnish I check 'em again and test 'em. My label is the last thing to go in, and the instrument will be second to none. That's how you make a reputation in this business, and we're damned good at what we do.'

'This description is so at odds with everything that has been passed down through the centuries about you and your work.'

'Such as?'

'We all believe that the superiority of your violins is an impenetrable mystery. Some say it is a secret varnish; others cite arcane preparation of the wood...'

'Balls! We buy the wood from the dealers like everyone else—of course I'm very picky—and the varnish is what all of us use, woodworkers, cabinetmakers, you name 'em. Superiority comes because they're so well made. And because I'm damned good at my trade.'

'People in my era say they can tell a Stradivarius from any other violin by the character of its sound.'

'Balls again. They're shitting you. If I shut my eyes, I can't tell one from another, and I make the damned things. Nobody could. Mind you, I could tell you *who* was playing!'

'I have here some examples of your work which I have brought with me from... the place where I come from. Would you be so kind as to take a look?'

'Gladly. It'll be like meeting old friends.'

'Pass me my case again, please. Now this one is prized as a very fine example of your middle period.'

'Hmm... That's a nice back—I could see us doing that—and the front's a good piece of wood, but what's all this other nonsense? Somebody has really buggered around with this. Look, the arching's far too high—must have steamed it—you've got the neck angle wrong, and it's a new one anyway, and this fingerboard is far too long. And what's with these strings? Bet they've pissed around with the innards too.'

'But surely you would agree that this violin was made in your workshop.'

'Well, the front and back, sure. Ribs, likely. But the rest... Mind if I play it?'

'Absolutely you can! Imagine! Me hearing the great Antonio Stradivari playing one of his own violins!'

'I'm not all that good, but here goes ... No, no, no! I can't play anymore, sorry. This is awful!'

'What's wrong with it?'

'It's like nothing that ever came out of here. What *have* you done? *Roberto!* Come back in here, and bring one of the Lisboa batch that's been strung up. And I need more rosin.'

'There are violinists in my era who would give their eye teeth for a chance to play one of these, and no serious professional can be without a Cremona. I have to say I am rather disappointed.'

'Well, listen to one fresh from the shop floor. Thanks Roberto ... Is that not the sweetest sound?'

'It's lovely, but it's a very... er, small sound, if you know what I mean? We're used to much greater power...'

'That's why yours has been buggered around I suppose. Wrong neck, high tension; of course you'd get it louder, but look what you lose! Think *you're* disappointed? *I'm* disappointed! This is like meeting a childhood friend who's grown up to get palsy or gone blind. It's a tragedy. Why would they do this?'

'In my era there are large orchestras, huge auditoriums. Power is essential.'

'I get it, but why fart around with an old one when you can make a new one? It doesn't make any sense.'

'It's your enormous reputation that drove the changes.'

'Well, it's ill-gotten and downright embarrassing. Gratifying to know, but hardly earned when these things sound nothing like a Stradivari. Odd sort of world you come from.'

'May I show you another? This one is from the 1660s, your earlier period.'

'Hmm. Nice to know these things survived, eh? Even though ruined. Let's see... Hmm... No, I don't recognize any of this. Not a bit. The other one had a front and back that we could have done, but there's nothing here.'

'Having produced so many, how can you be sure?'

'I told you; I'm damned good at what I do. This isn't one of ours. Cremona, yes, but look at the way this rib curves. We wouldn't have done it like that. Ever.'

'It does have your label in it.'

'Oh, anybody can stick a label in. One time there was some cheeky bastard apprentice stealing his boss's labels. I've heard he empties tosspots for loose change these days.'

An Interview in York Castle

'Do you know who I am?'

'No, and I give less 'n a bishop's fart. I want no confessor, if that's what you are.'

'I am here neither to take confession nor to console.'

'Who are you? Somebody musta slipped me somethin'. You ain't there.'

'I am indeed present. I have come from far away to interview Dick Turpin, the great popular hero and romantic blade before he goes to the gibbet.'

'I don't want no interviewing. I'm for the noose and there's an end to it.'

'I know you are condemned to die, but in kindness, I do trust that your end will be swift.'

'Nah, they don't go for long droppers at Knavesmire. They hang yer low. Yer don't break yer neck; yer strangle.'

'But that's a hideous fate for a such a hero as yourself!'

'Hero? Me? Still, I got an easy out. Yer pays a couple of street urchins a silver sixpence to jump up and grab yer legs.'

'Well, before you meet this awful fate, let me at least praise your valour and daring. We should dwell together upon your brave exploits before your sad execution.'

'Sad? Why sad? Dint I have it coming? I was born to be hung. I've robbed and murdered and raped me way through half of England.'

'The legends, songs and recountings tell a far different story. "Turpin, that mischievous blade". I wish you could have heard all the songs and poems of praise, read the books. To a great many people over the centuries, you've become a hero who robbed from the wealthy, gave to the poor, and resisted the long arms of authority and the law. A character larger than life.'

'Must be thinking of some other cove. Give to the poor?! Me? Hah! I took whatever I could off of whoever I could. Give to the poor, my horse's arse!'

'But the tales tell of a valiant figure fighting for the poor and disadvantaged against cruel authority.'

'Not me. Somebody else. I'm shite through and through. Shot me own pal in room of a sheriff, got copped for shooting a rooster. Read the fuckin' court records!'

'But did you not make that heroic ride on Black Bess?'

'Black who? I don't recall riding no black called Bess.'

'No, no, Black Bess was your horse.'

'Oh, was she? So, I was supposed to have given a name to horse? I don't name 'em; I steal 'em. Ain't nuthin' to do with me. Piss off!'

'I refer to your desperate ride from Essex to York. So, what horse did you saddle for that heroic ride?'

'What are you on about? Horses and Essex and York. They've slipped me something…'

'The tale is told that in order to establish an alibi for a crime you were accused of, you rode from Essex to York in one night.'

'Where is this shite coming from?'

'Perhaps I could read you a passage?

> The towers and pinnacles of York burst upon him in all the freshness, the beauty, and the glory of a bright, clear, autumnal morn…
>
> 'It is done—it is won,' cried Dick. 'Hurrah! hurrah!' And the sunny air was cleft with his shouts.
>
> Bess was not insensible to her master's exultation. She neighed feebly in answer to his call, and reeled forwards. It was a piteous sight to see her—to mark her staring, protruding eyeball—her shaking flanks; but, while life and limb held together, she held on.
>
> Another mile is past. York is near.
>
> 'Hurrah!' shouted Dick; but his voice was hushed. Bess tottered—fell. There was a dreadful gasp—a parting moan—a snort; her eye gazed, for an instant, upon her master, with a dying glare; then grew glassy, rayless, fixed. A shiver ran through her frame. Her heart had burst.'

'You finished? This is fuckin' nuts. Would ha' killed the nag before Cambridge for Christ's sake.'

'Yes, Dick, but look how heroically this story has been told! This is the *real* you.'

'I think you're as fuckin' mad as some of the people in here. Who put together this codswallop?'

'There's more. What about *The Ballad of Dick Turpin*? Here are some of the words:

On Hounslow Heath as I rode o'er
I spied a lawyer riding before.
"Kind sir," said I, "are you afraid,
Of Turpin, that mischievous blade?"

Said Turpin, "He'd ne'er find me out
I hid my money in my boot".
The lawyer says, "There's none can find,
I hid my gold in my cape behind".

And the chorus goes "Oh rare Turpin hero, Oh rare Turpin Oh". You see! You tricked the lawyer into revealing where he kept his gold. Now that's crafty. Not a bad exploit for a swashbuckling highwayman, eh?'

'It don't figure. Here's this dirty, pock-marked piece of human garbage what never did no one any good—and all ready for trussin' up—and here are you trumpin' me up as a hero.'

'That's what you've become in the popular eye.'

'What popular eye?'

'Over time, tales get told and legends are created. You are the lucky recipient of dame history's selective tradition. Good has been created, bad has been relegated.'

'So, this murdering piece of filth is now a hero. That it?'

'A popular hero, yet. Absolutely. In the place where I come from, several centuries hence, we carry parallel incompatible stories. We have lost the value of truth; narrative has become relativistic.'

'What the...?'

'On the popular level you are a likeable romantic hero leading a life of honour and chivalry. However, should any of us choose to dig deeper they would discover the full, vile infamy. I choose to believe and hold to the former.'

'But they look at the court records, they find out what a piece of shit I really was?'

'Yes, but no. That knowledge will not supplant or displace the romantic image. You will be the one, you will be the other, and you will be both.'

'Where the fuck are you takin' me with this?'

'Here's my advice. Just an eyeblink before those street urchins seize you round the knees, make your choice.'

Tea with the Earl of Oxford

It's a strange decoction, but not unpleasant.'

'It is very popular in my time. It's the leaves of the tea bush, especially prepared and steeped in hot water. We bring it from India and Cathay.'

'We have similar: chamomile and such herbs. Why do you say this is so popular?'

'It contains a substance called caffeine, which people find habit-forming.'

'Ah, like the great problem with this Virginia tobacco leaf presently. There is a miasma which beguiles, so perhaps it is so with this tea.'

'Yes. In my day many substances of this kind are used for pleasure.'

'You say your "time" and your "day". When exactly is your "day"?'

'That's a little hard to express. Let's just say it is elsewhen, and leave it at that.'

'I suppose it's no less believable than Edward de Vere, 17th Earl of Oxford is both in his grave and sitting with you in a study in an Oxford college drinking this… tea.'

'Exactly. So, let's put credulity aside for a while. Now, I invited you to my rooms because I am a researcher and student of the literature of the Elizabethan and Jacobean eras.'

'I may have been the Earl of Oxford, but I was scarcely ever here. At Court in London is where I was usually found.'

'Quite so. Your title and my college are mere happenstance, but I would like you to help me explore a conundrum that has puzzled scholars for centuries. To wit, the true identity of William Shakespeare.'

'Oh, the man Shakespeare, the London playwright?'

'Yes, exactly. I have come to you because you, of all people, would know the true origin of his works.'

'Me? Surely, would you not ask about in London where he lived and worked?'

'Come along. Just between the two of us. It need go no further.'

'What *are* you talking about?'

'We all know there was a vow of silence; secrecy among you courtly poets.'

'Secrecy? Hardly. We exchanged our poetry quite openly, and we aired our works publicly. I, myself, had a couple of dozen poems published and, modesty aside, I was ranked first among the courtly poets by none other than Webb and Puttenham. But what of it?'

'I mean about plays.'

'Oh, plays! I wrote masques and plays for my troupes, Oxford's Boys and Oxford's Men, but none that I would rank highly. They existed only in manuscript, and I certainly never published them, for they were ephemera suited merely to time and place. I would not be known to posterity as a coarse playwright.'

'I refer more to the plays of Shakespeare.'

'What of them?'

'Their authorship.'

'To the best of my knowledge, the man himself is their author. How would it be otherwise?'

'Let me overcome your coyness and come to the point. It is widely known that you are, in fact, the true author of Shakespeare's plays...'

'*I? I am their author?* You must be mad!'

'Between the two of us and these four walls, I see no reason why you should deny it.'

'Because it is utterly false! How could I? The man is prodigious and has a genius I could never emulate. You flatter me, sir.'

'Oh, come now, it's no flattery. You are the most excellent poet, master of many forms, a perfect candidate.'

'I *do not* write dramas for the world's consumption, let alone lay claim to those by another and superior hand.'

'Many scholars, not just I, have come to this conclusion. How can you argue against it?'

'Only that it is utterly without foundation.'

'We have devised lists of features and incidents in your life that are reflected accurately in the texts of Shakespeare's plays. Our proofs are solid.'

'If anyone were to write a million words, I doubt not that someone with a great deal of time on his hands could draw such lists of coincidences. Let's speak rather of facts.'

'Our evidence is more than convincing, were you just to look at some of the instances. I would be obliged if you were to give me your views. Let me cite one example: the name Shakespeare is clearly a pseudonym. It is taken to refer to Athena, goddess of the arts and learning, because she is often depicted shaking a spear.'

'*Shaking* a spear? Does that not imply movement? I know of no painting or sculpture that shakes of its own accord, save for the tremors I once experienced in Napoli. Are we speaking, then, of depictions set in motion by clock-work, or other hidden device? Surely, would not Holdspear or Brandishspear serve better?'

'Perhaps a better example? Shakespeare often writes of Italy in his dramas, although he never visited there, while you are a regular traveller.'

'Does the man not speak with others in taverns? Does the man not read books? This is trivial.'

'Taken together, the coincidences are impressive…'

'No, I'll have no more of William Pointspear. Now tell me; have you ever written a play?'

'No. I have not. I am a scholar, not a practitioner.'

'It would behoove you to try it, for you can have no idea of the actual craft of writing for the theatre until you have done it. How long would it take, for instance, to write out by hand just one of Wagglespear's plays? Just one. And then to write out the parts severally so that all players may memorize their lines?'

'I really couldn't say…'

'Or the instructions to the backstage, the costumes, the properties, music.'

'As I say, it's not within my experience.'

'That is evident. Sitting at your desk in an Oxford college how could it be? Dip a quill into an inkhorn and try it. Do you believe, sir, that there would be enough time in my entire life to write *but one* of his works let alone the gamut? All this amidst my military services in Holland and during the Spanish nonsense, my visits to Italy—of which you are manifestly aware—and my extensive duties to the Court.'

'I agree, you would be a very busy man…'

'I would neither sleep, nor eat, nor fornicate. How many plays are there ascribed to his hand?'

'We know of at least 38. I have here a list in chronological order, which I was hoping you would be able to verify.'

'Hmm. You know of course that I left this mortal coil by agency of the plague in 1604, whereas Shakespeare lived until 1616.'

'Yes, I was hoping we could discuss that little issue…'

'I'm sure you were. Give me the list. Hmm, let's look here. You were going to ask me how I had written: *Measure for Measure, King Lear, Macbeth, Antony and Cleopatra, Coriolanus, Timon of Athens, Pericles, Cymbeline, The Winter's Tale, The Tempest, Henry VIII, The Two Noble Kinsmen* and *The Winter's Tale*, while yet mouldering in the grave. Well, by what agency was this magic brought about?'

'Scholars have debated this flaw in our reasoning, and we argue that these supposed later works were actually written pre-mortem.'

'Why, of course! Certainly easier than animating a corpse to perform the task. And not so noisome. So, being vouchsafed a premonition of my forthcoming demise—which no mortal has ever yet been granted—I took the time to produce what you would call, I think, a stockpile of… let's see… 13 dramas. And all this on top of my writing and producing the plays of Shakespeare that were being staged while I was yet aboveground.'

'When you put it that way… I must say that, being in

your presence and hearing your side of the affair, we might well need to reassess our conclusions.'

'Well you might! You might also ask yourself why it is so essential to assign the writings of some crude, ill-educated Warwickshire yokel to a courtly man of class and sophistication. Have you forgotten the determining factor of inborn genius?'

'No, of course not.'

'To the contrary, I believe you have quite forgotten. You know of Michelangelo, I don't doubt.'

'Naturally. The whole world does.'

'Yes, a coarse stone quarrier's brat from Settignano. I am sure that if you and your ilk were able, you would be pleased to wrest his chisels and brushes from his hands and assign his work to a man of culture and sophistication. Now, would you mind sending me back to the place from whence you called me? Your company is cloying.'

A Meeting in a Gallery at The Globe

Do you know where you are?'

'This is *The Globe*, by God, but it's like no *Globe* I ever knew.'

'Your *Globe* is long since gone, but this one rose phoenix-like from its ashes.'

'Explain yourself.'

'You are a shade that I have conjured from wherever you reside. *The Globe* was rebuilt by generous donation from the New World, which is now a prosperous place of great industry.'

'And you have brought me here to show me this?'

'In part. I thought to bring you to familiar surroundings to lessen the shock. Will you stay with me if I tell you that we are 400 and more years into your future?'

'Do you offer me an option? Do you think I sit here by choice?'

'No, I don't believe you do, but I would not have you here on sufferance.'

'I'm willing enough. Proceed.'

'I have an important quest. Your genius echoes down the centuries. You stand head and shoulders above any of your contemporaries and predecessors. The sheer number and quality of your works has astonished generations.'

'Hmm, do I detect just a hint of flattery?'

'I'm telling you only the truth.'

'So, what of it? I knew from the cradle that I was destined to shake the world. It is self-evident that no man ever came close to my prodigious production, and I knew as I grew up in Stratford, and worked in London on play after play that I had laid down a legacy that would stand for ever.'

'Modesty being your strong suit?'

'Just so. But you are neither here to praise nor to flatter, although neither one nor the other would hardly stick. You know my story, you know my works, so what more do you want of me?'

'A great deal, if you can indulge me. You see, there are

those amongst us who question the authorship of your works…'

'That they were written by another? Hah! There surely could not have been another as committed, as driven, and as accomplished as I. We are not two a penny, you know. Who would presume so?'

'There are many scholars who assign your work to others. Among the possibilities we find William Stanley, Sir Roger Manners, Francis Bacon, Christopher Marlowe, Edward de Vere … it's a long list.'

'How dare they! How dare they try to wrest my works from me!'

'No, no, they didn't. It is posterity that has cast questions. It's a matter of documentation.'

'Documentation? Sifting through papers? Hmm… True, when I passed on, I did leave a dreadful mess. God bless Heminges and Condell, the King's Men, and those of the Stationers Company who set things to rights. The *First Folio* is a masterpiece, and when I think of the multitude of poorly printed quartos that were sold under my name, the sheaves of papers, copies, overwritten notes that my shelves in Stratford and London were stuffed with, I am in awe of their energy and dedication. I was too damned busy while still enjoying the flowers from above.'

'So, from your elevated position in the Hereafter, you would endorse the *First Folio?*'

'Absolutely! It encompasses my major dramas in a detail and completeness that I would have thought impossible. To produce it so few years after my demise was a heroic and selfless undertaking.'

'I would agree, of course, but more to the point, you would attest that the works are all of your authorship?'

'As I have told you, there was no other mortal who could have done what I did. I stood alone on a pinnacle of achievement. So be damned to any who would steal my fame!'

'Among those many candidates I mentioned, Edward de Vere, 17th Earl of Oxford, stands out.'

'*What!? Edward!* Oh, dear me, no! Surely, these copyright thieves could produce a better man than that, could they not? They winnowed their list down to *this?*'

'Not a worthy candidate?'

'Have you read his attempts at the playwright's craft?'

'No plays by Edward de Vere himself have survived, alas, so it's impossible to judge.'

'Scarce surprising. His attempts at the play were dreadful. I don't doubt the pages were used to warm his household once Oxford's Men had performed them. Not worth the labour of printing, even by the botchers and swindlers who egested quarto chapbooks like swine slop.'

'So, in your opinion he is not likely to have written your works under a pseudonym?'

'No, indeed. And under what pseudonym, pray?'

'William Shakespeare…'

'… Oh, thank God, this shade you have invoked is capable of laughter! What's in a name? An Edward by any other name would write as sweet. Or foul. Oh, hold my splitting sides.'

'Let me give you a minute to recover yourself.'

'That's better. Mirth is such wonderful fuel for the soul (which is what I suppose I am). But, you know, de Vere was so enamoured of the drama that we would often meet, clandestinely of course, for a courtly gentleman would not wish it bruited about that he consorted with coarse playwrights.'

'You actually *knew* Edward de Vere?'

'As I say. We met often. I have to confess that, as a travelled man of the world, and one with high literary connections, I wasn't loath to… pump him, as I think you would say. I eat and drink books; always have. He had many.'

'There are arguments amongst us that you could not have written in so much detail about Italy, having never visited.'

'Arr, tha's roight! Coun'ry bumpkins from Warwickshire doan't travel to furrun places. But, it's child's play to get the gist, and only a fool would think to check details. And find them wanting. *The Merchant of Venice, Romeo and Juliet, Two Gentlemen of Verona*... why the list goes on and on. 'Tis imagination, all of it, and not for bookish lawyers to pore over. It is to be strutted on the stage and believed for its intrinsic worth.'

'I agree wholeheartedly. Then there is the problem of de Vere's early death.'

'Aye, death is a problem for all of us. I am here before you to attest to that, although this too-temporary corporeal reality becomes me rather well, think you not?'

'I mean that he predeceased you by some 12 years. The arguments are that he wrote the later plays ascribed to you during his lifetime.'

'Really? I think I might probably have noticed him doing it. Oh, stay! I remember now! Shortly after his death, I received at my house a vast bundle of papers from him. It contained 13 dramas, all nicely writ out in parts with directions for staging, and all neatly tied in twine. He even specified the order in which they should be performed. From 1604 onward, I knew I could rest on my laurels and not write another damned word.'

'Ah, you're making a comedy of this interview.'

'What do you expect of such a stupid argument? Is it not already a comedy?'

'Well, bringing you here has laid all my doubts to rest. Edward de Vere, 17th Earl of Oxford, was the most likely candidate among our scholars who wished for anybody but William Shakespeare to have written your oeuvre. Their claim for him is dead in my eyes.'

'In your eyes? So, in this place where you live, my good name will still be under attack? Have I not given you my assurance?'

'Of course I have it, but why would they ever believe

me? You, sir, are a figment of my imagination. "I have spoken to The Bard of Avon himself, and he assures me that he is the author of the works ascribed to him in the *First Folio*". That would go down well…'

'Aye, they would think you mad. Seems that invoking my spirit has served only you.'

'Take solace in this: in this age you see around you—although its full horror is screened by this simulacrum of *The Globe*—there are those who would create conspiracies and subterfuges for the sport of it. They comb libraries and archives, and spin hypotheses and suppositions among themselves. They sit at desks, they lecture students, they produce learnèd papers. But they have never, themselves, been involved with the craft of the playwright, and that is the fatal flaw in all their reasoning.'

'And the truth is there for all to see and hear on yon boards. I am William Shakespeare; there is no other.'

'Ahh, truth…'

A Penetrating Conversation

It's a hell of a journey south through the mountains. I had no idea it would be so dark and gloomy. And I had to walk up from the gate.'

'Ah, you must be soaked. The Carpathians experience almost continual thunder and lightning, relieved a little by impenetrable fogs, as you would know from the movies. Welcome, pleased to meet you; let me take your cape, hang it by the fire. Name's Vlad.'

'Yes. Vlad the Impaler, I understand.'

'There you go! As soon as you walk in my door! It's not fair! I get called the Impaler all the time, just 'cuz I did it a couple of times. If you were caught pissing behind a tree, would you be Robert the Pisser for the rest of your life?'

'That would be a little unfair, I suppose. After all, Ethelred was only unready once.'

'Well, unreedy really, but I get your point. What I'm saying is Pepin the Short was always short, right? Eric the Red was always red, but Vlad the Impaler? I think the record's biased in favour of the impalees.'

'Well, that's why I'm here. I am a pan-temporal record examiner, getting the inside story on myth and legend. However, there is always historical fact to take into account.'

'Historical *what?*'

'Fact. There was the small matter of Târgovişte in 1462.'

'Never heard of it. Have a seat. Here, let me pour you a glass of this excellent Hungarian wine. I get it from my good friend Count Dracula. He has an agent in Budapest.'

'I wasn't... this is *very* good wine... about to discuss another Dracula...'

'Did you meet him on your way here?'

'I'm confused. Isn't that your family name, anyway?'

'No, different guy. He's fictional; I'm real. We cross the fact/fiction boundary line a lot here in the remote Carpathians. I think it's due to the incessant thunder. Didn't meet him, then?'

'I didn't have that pleasure. Look, I want to...'

'He's a gentleman is Dracula. We have these Open Castles

in these parts, y'know, so we can go visit each other's crag-poised gothic retreats. Smooth feller he is; urbane, sophisticated… as long as you meet him at night.'

'Yes, I heard that he was particularly lucifugous…'

'Yeah, and he hates the light too. Batshit crazy about the sun. And there's always problems with armies of peasants carrying torches, armed with pikes and pitchforks bashing on his doors. Enough to put anyone off ruling a territory.'

'Speaking of ruling, you, as the ruler of Wallachia, *this* territory…'

'Tell you what, though. I think Christopher Lee did him best. Did you see that movie? The Hammer Films one? Along with Peter Cushing as Dr van Helsing. Jeez, they should've had an Oscar, the pair of them.'

'But, back to Târgoviște…'

'Name rings a bell. Here, have another glass. Oh, look, your cape's dry now. Let me get Igor to show you to your room. You must be tired after a long drive in that rattly old carriage. Did the coachman say anything?'

'He didn't say a word.'

'Taciturn doesn't begin to describe Carpathian coachmen. Not sure if they're even living beings, frankly. Finished your wine? Good. *Igor!* Come and show the gentleman to the east wing. And stop saying "Yeth, mathter" like that. You know how to speak properly; you're just doing it for show.'

'But really, before I go to bed, I *did* want to clear up a few matters.'

'Oh, my Lord, just look at the time!'

'I must insist we speak. *Now!*'

'Oh… all right then. What about?'

'I suppose you've forgotten what the Ottoman army found after your retreat from Târgoviște in 1462. You told me you'd never heard of it.'

'I have this memory thing, you know. I really should be able to remember, shouldn't I? I'm seeing somebody about it. Regularly.'

'Yes, you should. Remember, I mean. Your army had abandoned Târgoviște, as I'm sure you'll soon recall. The Sultan's army found an area of impalements, which was 100 feet by 40 feet. The Ottomans figured about 20,000 men, women, and children had been spitted.'

'Okay, okay. It's a fair cop. I remember now! You've got me bang to rights. But there's no way it was that many. Get a pen and paper and do the math. Somebody must have thrown in an extra couple of zeros. I mean, look at it: you'd never pack that many into that space. That's exactly what I mean by impalee bias!'

'No matter the number, it does imply that the epithet is justified.'

'Not really. I could be Vlad the Great, or Vlad the Wise, or plain old Vlad III Drăculești. It's not fair.'

'Well, history has recorded the epithet, and it's not possible to undo it. "Not all thy piety or wit could cancel half a line, nor all they tears wash out a word of it".'

'Okay, I've heard of Omar Khayaam; I'm not that ignorant. Bullshitting me with erudition. But you know what? The Sultan was amazed. He said "It was not possible to deprive of his country a man who had done such great deeds, who had such a diabolical understanding of how to govern his realm and its people", so there! You've got to be tough in the Carpathians, or it's the peasants and the flaming torches.'

'Nevertheless, how does the Sultan's appreciation of your barbarity mitigate the act, or ameliorate the epithet?'

'Listen. He said: "A man who had done such things was worth much", and he knew a thing or two about ruling. Here, let me fill your glass.'

'Thank you, no. The argument remains that...'

'But you have to remember I'm a Roman Catholic, so things like that are okay with the church as long as no Catholics are spitted. It's all heretics and heathens and such that need lessons taught. People like me are a divine driving force, and even unbelievers like the Sultan see the sense in that.'

'You know, I really think it is time for bed.'

'Sleep tight, then. See you at breakfast. Igor roasted two peasants today.'

'Pheasants?'

'No peasants. On a spit…'

Drinking Wine with Boudica

'This is very fine stuff! Quite a change from a lifetime of Roman horse piss.'

'I'm glad you like it. It's from Gaul; France as it is now.'

'Hmm. Pour me some more.'

'There. So, Boudica, I'm so pleased you could take the time for a little chat.'

'Be glad to. My name's not Boudica, by the way, but I'll let you use it. It means Victory in Brythonic, so it's really quite appropriate. Well, in the beginning, anyway…'

'I love the gold necklace and that beautifully coloured tunic, by the way. It's exactly as Cassius Dio described it.'

'Yes, it becomes me. Indeed, I went to my funeral pyre wearing it. Thought it would be appropriate to wear it for this visit from The Halls.'

'And the mantle and the brooch go so well with your flowing, waist-length hair.'

'If you're trying flattery, forget it. You want me to give, lay off.'

'Oh, no, not at all. I was really just reflecting on what Dio wrote. He said that this was your invariable attire.'

'What the hell would a man know about my "invariable attire", especially a Roman? And he wasn't even there. Speaking of which, it would be nice to know what you've heard about me, your sources being somewhat biased. There's a lot of stuff needs setting right.'

'Well, your popular reputation is second to none. You are regarded as a female icon, fighting and dying gloriously in freeing your people from oppression. You know, the usual: Imperialist yoke, Roman heel.'

'That's nice and heartwarming, but then there's the written version.'

'True. The Roman point of view is all we have: *Agricola* and *Annals* by Tacitus, something from Suetonius in his *Lives of the Caesars*, and an account of your revolt in Dio's *History of the Empire*. That's why I've asked you here.'

'Shoot.'

'The story really starts with the rebellion of your tribe the Iceni, does it not?'

'No. Long before. When the Romans conquered Britain, all the tribal kings became their vassals and were disarmed. My husband Esuprastus, may the gods piss on his memory, signed off our kingdom in his will to the Emperor Nero and our two daughters.'

'I thought Prasutagus, the king of the Iceni, was your husband.'

'There you go. Typical mistake from a Roman writer who wasn't even there! If Tacitus couldn't even get my husband's bloody name right, what's the hope for him giving an unbiased account?'

'So Esuprastus gave over the kingdom to be co-owned by your daughters and the emperor?'

'Yes, insane you'll agree. Notice I don't figure; I'm only the queen after all.'

'Our historians have always thought this was an unusual arrangement, to say the least.'

'Unusual? Oh, how very observant! Madness, I call it. But what do you do when you've got a Roman sword across your windpipe? Yes sir, no sir, show me where to sign sir.'

'So, after his death the will was ignored?'

'Ignored... Words like integrity, honour, justice, probity, honesty spring to my mind. Yes, ripped into shreds and shat on. Decianus Catus, the Procreator, annexed the whole kingdom; they pillaged and burned, they stole our property, raped my daughters, and flogged me half to death. Want me to show you the scars?'

'No, no, I believe you! Please continue.'

'Then all the donations Imperial Rome had made were confiscated, and that bastard Seneca called in the loans that had been imposed at spear's point. So, impoverished, abused, lied to, cheated. We were, quite literally, fucked.'

'So, a rebellion of the Iceni must have been inevitable.'

'Of course. You would know this from your own time,

wouldn't you? You oppress an entire people for decades, treat them like dirt, the boil is going to burst.'

'Surely, Decianus Catus must have seen the uprising coming.'

'Not him. You have to understand that Britan was on the outer edge of the empire, so the least able people were assigned here. If you were some Roman patrician with ambitions, would you want to be sent to the bitter edge of the known world? You know, the fogs, the damp, the continual rain, long winters, people always whining about the weather; it's a horrible country, and I was born here! Imperial Britain was staffed by riff-raff. Then, this idiot Catus decided to barge in while Governor Suetonius, the only halfway competent man in the entire province, was off thrashing the Druids in Ynys Môn.'

'What's now known as Anglesea.'

'Right. Without Suetonius in the south, these complacent idlers had left themselves completely open, and unbeknownst to them we'd been arming for some time.'

'You saw it coming?'

'Damn right we did. Only a moron would take a Roman at his word, and that so-called will smelt of garbage before the ink was dry.'

'In his *History of the Empire*, Cassius Dio gives you a beautiful speech where you incite your people to rebellion.'

'Yes, I've seen it. Oh, it's a lovely, flowery piece of writing. Highly eloquent and creative and, give him his due, he sums it up perfectly: oppression, taxation, servitude, slavery. Complete fabrication, of course. I would never have said all that stuff because everybody knew it anyway. I remember exactly what I did say when I had all the warrior chiefs of the Iceni and the Trinovantes into my tent.'

'Yes…?'

'Let's destroy these bastards! And we did.'

'And Camulodunum was your first target.'

'Easy pickings there. They'd kicked the Trinovantes out

of the town and settled a bunch of their retired soldiers there. Almost no resistance; scarcely a garrison. We sacked the place totally and drove the populace out. The Trinovantes were only too happy to come back and help.'

'The records show that your rebels butchered men, women and children indiscriminately.'

'Absolute lies! Roman propaganda. And stop calling us rebels. We were freedom fighters.'

'And you set fire to the Temple of Claudius where the populace had taken refuge.'

'More lies! They also wrote that we had 120,000 fighting men. Ridiculous. There weren't that many men who could bear arms in the entire province. They'd write anything to make themselves look better than they were.'

'I'm so glad I've had you here to clarify some of these things. Some more wine?'

'Thanks; need it. But, of course, they had to tell the truth about Petilius Cerialis, didn't they? Couldn't gloss over that one.'

'The failed attempt to relieve Camulodunum?'

'Poor bugger only had a handful of auxiliaries. I don't think we left one of them alive. Then it was on to Londinium and Verulamium. Meanwhile, that cretin Decianus Catus fled to Gaul. Hope he died in misery.'

'Tacitus reports that in the sacking of Londinium and Verulamium at least 80,000 people were killed. The rebe... er, freedom fighters, he says, were not interested in preserving the lives of the Roman population, but slaughtered them by hanging, burning and crucifixion.'

'There! See! You've caught them in a lie! We had never heard of crucifixion—how could we?—so that's clearly false.'

'So, just hangings and burnings then?'

'Hey, whose side are *you* on? You're supposed to be impartial. As if we'd be butchering innocent people! The very idea.'

'So, no hangings or burnings either?'

'All right… there might have been a few. You know how it is… Relieving their souls of the burden of their bodily restraints.'

'Quite. Even so, history has cut you a bit of slack in view of your righteous anger. Perspective, if not forgiveness.'

'Gimme another glass. You're opening old wounds.'

'Speaking of which, there was the final battle along Watling Street…'

'That coward Suetonius had to hurry back from Ynys Môn, but he took one look at Londinium and let it burn. Didn't dare face us, the yellow bastard. He had to bide his time before putting together a force big enough to take us on.'

'Tacitus says the Romans were hopelessly outnumbered.'

'Another whopping lie. He says Suetonius was supposed to have been facing 230,000, and beat us handily with his 10,000. That, sir, is complete Roman bullshit. The victors always inflate the numbers, but that one's beyond laughable.'

'But you *were* defeated.'

'We were defeated by Roman strategy. We never had strategy; we only had anger. And by the time he faced us our anger was ashes. Win the battle or perish, that's what I told my people.'

'And you perished…'

'By all accounts it was a lavish funeral. This tunic, my robe, my gold. Fabulous!'

'So, the biggest question of all then: Tacitus says you poisoned yourself; Cassius Dio says you fell sick and died. Which was it?'

'Really excellent, this wine. Cheers!'

On Patmos with John

'Who are you?'

'What do you mean, who am I? I'm Prester John.'

'Yes, but who *is* Prester John?'

'Depends who you ask.'

'Elaborate please.'

'It might be a pleasure to do so, but first of all I want to know what the hell I'm doing here. You've just whipped me out of Up There without so much as a by-your-leave.'

'Fair point. It's not a gift I can easily explain, but I have the ability to call forth historical or mythical figures and to interview them, either in my time period or in theirs. I thought a beach shelter on Patmos, with a glass of retsina and a bowl of nuts at your elbow, would provide a suitable ambience for recollection.'

'So, there you go! Depends who you ask, I said, didn't I? Well, you've got the wrong John.'

'I have to admit I did have some trouble with multiple Johns in my research.'

'Right on! There are more Johns than at a triathlon transition, and they're just as portable.'

'So, you are not John of Patmos?'

'No way! I *did not* write *Revelation*. That was some other John, sunning himself on a beach with a quill and ink, and using some most excellent mushrooms, I should add. Have you read that thing? Wow!'

'So, could you elaborate on who you are, please?'

'Difficult, as I'm largely mythical. That's the trouble with scholars in general; they write things, they read things, they draw conclusions, they invent stuff, and bits go missing, then someone comes along later and confuses, interpolates and postulates, and every century it happens all over again. The truth gets pushed even further away in a welter of mythologizing, speculation, duplication and confusion. Before you know it, Wikipedia is a mass of totally irreconcilable data, a tangled mess of hyperlinks, and you need a degree in medieval eastern European history to sort it all out.'

'For an early medieval cultural figment, you seem to know a great deal about our modern world.'

'I don't see things in a linear way Up There; more like a continuum really. Imagine Tralfamadorians or Billy Pilgrim.'

'Ah, I see. Or, no, I don't… Perhaps we could drill down to some facts about you?'

'Facts! Hah!'

'Well, the non-mythical bits, anyway.'

'Hmm, tough. Okay, I was invented in the 11th century by Bishop Hugh of Gebel in Syria. This was in the middle of the Crusades when half of Europe was invading the Holy Land. Hugh sent a report about me to the Papal Court saying I was a Christian ruler in India—which was a highly flexible geographical location in those days—and that I'd come to aid the forces wresting Palestine from the Infidel. Unfortunately for fact, but fortunately for fiction, I was unable to get all the way to Jerusalem, being stopped at the crossing of the Tigris River. Had I made that crossing and marched south, I would have marched out of legend and into history.'

'So, your existence depends solely upon the words of Bishop Hugh?'

'And a river in flood without a bridge. But yes. His word was diluted further by the fact that Hugh's report was only written down by Bishop Otto of Freising, and he also claimed that I was descended from the Magi who attended the birth of the baby Jesus.'

'That *is* a bit of a historical stretch…'

'Is it ever! Would have been nice to know which one I was descended from, unless they were involved in a *menage a quatre*. Anyhow, you see how transparent I became by repetition.'

'And the name Prester John itself is shrouded in uncertainty.'

'Look at it this way: let's say if—and it's an enormous if, mind—my name was originally Gur-khan, or Kor-khan, which is the title of the Mongol Karakitai rulers… and assume said ruler is a Christian, and that ruler is me. Okay, so far? Good. Now, turn that phonetically into Hebrew, which gives you Yoḥanan, or into Syriac as Yuḥanan. So, then you haul that into Latin and presto, Johannes, and then John.'

'That's the "John", where's the Prester?'

'I was reputed to be a "king-priest", but in humility I preferred simply Prester, from "presbyter". I was the scion of a long Nestorian line that went back to the evangelizing journey of St Thomas, the doubting one.'

'He's not the only one...'

'See what happens when too many scholarly cooks spoil the historiographical broth?'

'Some of this is in the famous letter, isn't it?'

'Ah, thought you'd come to that. Infamous more like! In 1165 I wrote this letter to the Byzantine Emperor Manuel I Comnenus, cc'd to the Holy Roman Emperor Frederick I Barbarossa, and bcc'd to others. Don't remember writing it, but I'm a myth anyway. In it, the realm of Prester John is called "the three Indies", a land of miracles, peace, justice, you name it, overseen by priests and archbishops, with me at the top. It also says that I am guardian of the shrine of St Thomas, the apostle to India, at Mylapore. You see how nuts this has become?'

'But there *is* a shrine to St Thomas at Chennai in Tamil Nadu, isn't there?'

'Yes, the Portuguese "found" the burial site in the 16th century and built a church on top of it, but we're getting dragged away from the topic of "me" by hyperlinks, aren't we?'

'True. So, the letter...'

'Egregious forgery. It is astonishing what people would believe in those days. You heard the one about the True Cross? There's Constantine's mum digging around in the Holy Land, and coming back to Constantinople with the very baulk of timber on which Jesus Christ was crucified, all swathed in bubble-wrap! I mean, it makes my letter to Frederick I

Barbarossa—which I'm sure I didn't write, by the way—seem like a harmless jape.'

'Except that it provided a wonderful red herring for future commentators and scholars.'

'As did the later story that I was preaching away in Ethiopia, emperor of a Christian nation in East Africa. It's hellish being pulled in several directions at the same time; do you want me in India, do you want me in Mongolia, do you want me in Ethiopia!? Make your mind up, Clio! But you know what...?'

'No, what?'

'This may be excellent retsina, but I'm damned if I ever wrote anything while on Patmos.'

'Let me pour you some more. But where would we be if we had no scholarship, no lecterns, daises, pulpits, or ivory towers, no book-lined college snugs with pipe tobacco and tea? I think we'd be the poorer for it.'

'Of course we would. After all, I wouldn't be here without a whole load of well-meaning writers inventing me. Anything else I can tell you?'

'I think we've covered it completely. Well, look, it's been a real *Revelation* and a great pleasure to bring you here for this little talk.'

'Aspro pato!'

An Encounter in Sherwood Forest

'Ah, finally, I've found you! You must be the Robin Hood I've been seeking.'

'Well, me name's Hood and I do a bit of robbin'. What of it?'

'I've been wandering through Sherwood Forest for a long while hoping I would come across you.'

'Across me? Why me? I'm no one special. And who are you?'

'Difficult to explain, really. Let's say I am drawn by legends to meet the reality.'

'Yeah, and I'm the Queen of the fuckin' Fairies. I said, who are you?'

'Really I just want to sit down and talk with you.'

'*I know!* You're spying for the fucking Sheriff, aren't you? Well, you can piss off. I've got a man behind every tree, so you're a walking corpse. Scram!'

'Couldn't you just give me a few minutes? All I want to do is talk.'

'Oh, right! Yeah! Then go back to the Sheriff and tell him all about us! C'mon lads, let's string 'im up!'

'*Wait! Please!* I swear I'm not from the Sheriff. Tell your men to hold off. *Please!*'

'Keep your eyes on 'im. You. Sit on this log. This had better be good.'

'I guess I'm right in thinking these would be your merry men?'

'Merry?! You out of your mind? Whatever kind of merriment is there in skulking in the forest under sentence of hanging. Hilarious, that it is.'

'I mean, your band of outlaws.'

'Of course we're outlaws. Why do you think we're here? Appreciating nature in the big outdoors? Smelling the fucking bluebells?'

'But fighting against injustice, robbing from the rich to give to the poor, that sort of thing.'

'Oh, yeah, we do that for sure. Rob from the rich, eh, men? A sheep maybe, a couple of chickens, eggs.'

'And give to the poor?'

'Oh, yeah, we give to the poor, don't we lads?'

'I'm sorry, but why are you all cracking up laughing?'

'We give to *ourselves* you fool! Who could be poorer than us? No home, no work, no food, and living in filth among the trees.'

'Well, if you look at it that way… Er… I have to confess, I had expected you to be dressed in Lincoln green with a nice feather in your cap.'

''Stead of draped in rags and stinking like a midden, eh? No houses with walls and roofs around here, and we don't wash more'n once a year.'

'But your fight against injustice is real enough, of course. After all, it was the policies of King John that put you here.'

'King who? What king?'

'The king of England of course. The one whose harsh rule you are protesting with your campaigns.'

'We don't know nothing about kings, do we lads? Sheriff of Nottingham, he rules around here. Kings!'

'But you know that the rightful king of England is at war in the Holy Land, and that John is the usurper. That's why you lost your land.'

'Land? Me? I didn't lose no land 'cuz I never had any. Yeoman through and through. Ended up here because I stole two loaves of bread. Land! Right…'

'The story I have heard is that you were fighting with King Richard in the Holy Land, wresting Jerusalem from the Saracen infidel, and that when you returned you found you had been dispossessed.'

'Dispossessed? Hoo. Can't be dispossessed of nothing you never possessed in the first place.'

'You are Robin of Locksley, surely?'

'Told you, me name's Hood. Don't know what the hell you're talking about. C'mon, let's string him up!'

'*Wait, wait, wait!* Let me finish!'

'All right. Finish your fairy story then we'll decide what to do with you. It better be good.'

'In the version of the story I've been told you rebelled against authority, took refuge here in Sherwood Forest, and gathered about you a band of followers who fought for poor people against injustice.'

'So, this ragged bunch of scabby, pustulent, ulcerated scum you see before you are my "merry men", is that it?'

'Yes, yes! Then there's Friar Tuck, Little John, Will Scarlet, all standing beside you and equally skilled in weapons and combat. You, yourself, are an unparalleled archer.'

'Never shot an arrow in me life. You wanna catch coneys you're better trapping 'em with a snare. Any more tall yarns before we sling a rope over a tree?'

'There was Maid Marian, too, but she lived in the town, not in the forest…'

'*Maid* Marian? Har, har! There's no maids within a hundred miles of here that I know of. So, less see, this *Maid* Marian is this Robin Hood's piece, right?'

'Well, yes and no. She *was* his love interest. And she acted as a messenger, disguising herself and seeking him out in the forest. But they were never… you know… close like that.'

'Whoop-de-doo! Virgin meets virgin! Less sum up this precious cove of yours, shall we? He's landed gentry, he dresses in green with a feather in his cap, he has a band of merry men, the best archer in the shire, he steals from the rich and gives to the poor, and he has a virgin all panting for him but doesn't get into her kirtle. That about right?'

'When you put it like that…'

'I can put it however I like when your fuckin' neck's on the line.'

'But honestly, it's a wonderful story. Robin Hood is the romantic folk hero whom all people look up to. He is valiant, stalwart, honest and upright. He has all the manly virtues, none of the vices, and puts all others above himself. He is both chaste and virtuous. He returns from a selfless holy mission in a far land, only to find his birthright wrested from him by wicked injustice. He gathers about him a band of like-minded heroes and wages a campaign for those who are wronged and disenfranchised. What is *not* to like about this universal hero?'

'Where did you say you came from?'

'I didn't.'

'But it's that land, isn't it, where you've got a King John and this Richard, and things called Saracens, right?'

'Yes, it's England. Beyond the borders of Nottinghamshire…'

'Don't know nothing about borders. And your story of Robin Hood. That's me, right? Robbing Hood?'

'Well, yes. You're the hero I *thought* I was looking for.'

'So, that's what they say about me in this England of yours? Hero, eh?'

'Yes, and more besides. They also say that in the very near future King Richard the Lionhearted will return to his rightful kingdom, and all John's wickedness and injustices will be repaired. You will be free to return to the life you once knew.'

'Know what. The way you tell it, I kinda like this Robbing Hood cocksucker. Here's what I'll do: I'll have you stick around here and be our story teller. You can tell us all the stories of your Robbing Hood around the campfire, and the more you tell it, the more I'll be him. I think I might be able to dream myself into forgetting this filth and poverty and the vermin I'm forced to hang around with. Who knows, in hundreds of years it might become true. Story teller, eh? What d'ye say?'

'It's a very flattering offer, and in view of the, ah… *suspended* alternative…'

An Orchard in Fort Wayne, Indiana

JOHNNY APPLESEED.

Fort Wayne is a long way from where you were born.'

'Aye, I've travelled a bit over the years, sowing my seeds in more places than I can count. And now I'm near the end of God's allotted span.'

'You're famous of course—legendary even—but behind all the accumulated stories, I would like to find a deeper truth.'

'Deeper truth? What d'ye mean? What you see is what you get with Johnny Appleseed.'

'Yes, the simple clothes, the bare feet, and your beard and long hair. You've been taken as a symbol of the New Church; almost a prophet.'

'Bah! Certainly, I profess the faith of Swedenborg and I was never loath to tell people my views, but there's nothing special about me 'cept apples.'

'Let me go back to the beginning, if I may?'

'The beginning... Well, you know most of it anyway, do you not?'

'Yes, but, your single-minded campaign of planting apple seeds must have deep roots, if you'll pardon the allusion.'

'All right. I was born Johnathan Chapman in September, 1774. Of course, even as a young 'un I was taken with planting. See, after my mother died my father moved us from Leominster...'

'That's in Massachusetts, right?'

''Course. He moved to Longmeadow and married Lucy Cooley. Her son Nathaniel and me got on real well, even though he was younger than me by quite a bit. We worked the farm and we worked hard, and we learned a lot. I didn't like Lucy and she didn't like me. Dad was always, well... distant if you like, so Nathaniel and me took off and headed west. It may sound funny to you, but I was only 18 and Nathaniel 11, yet in 1792 off we went with no effort to stop us.'

'That's terribly young to head out on your own.'

'We were both of us canny about working the land for

sustenance, we knew how to live rough, and there was always farm work wherever you went.'

'There are stories that you first began cultivating apples in Pennsylvania around the time of the Whiskey Rebellion in 1794.'

'Yeah, and picking seeds out of the waste from the Potomac River cider mill! I dunno how people come up with this stuff. Sure, we were in Pennsylvania—a passel of places in the state when I first got interested in apples—but we ended up in Ohio when my father moved the family there.'

'But you didn't stay?'

'No. Nathaniel did, but I was after learning more about apples.'

'That's what I mean. It's this... focus, almost obsession if you like, with apples. I would like to dig into that.'

'Would you now? Well, you know of course that the apple is the prime symbol of our Fall. Every single apple we grow, every bite we take, is a reminder of our sin. But the apple beguiles us into externalizing sin. There is a great contest between our inner and our outer beings, and so we are constantly beguiled by material possessions and worldly recognition. Our actions are mere external displays which lack spiritual essence. We need always to see the deeper messages in the Bible, and live the pared-down essential life. We have lost Jesus Christ! We have lost *God!*'

'There's a story I read that you confronted a preacher with just this message.'

'And for once, they got it right. There was a preacher of the New Church—can't remember where it was—who said something like: "Find me a man like the primitive Christians, who travels to heaven barefooted and in coarse raiment". So, I walked right up to him and said, "Here's your primitive Christian"! That's how I live my life.'

'So, back to apples...'

'Well, I had an apprenticeship with an apple grower, Mr Crawford in Licking River, Ohio, and he really inspired me.

Mind you, he was doing a lot of grafting, which in my view is against God's law. The only worthy apple is one grown from seed.'

'Why is that?'

'The seed is simplicity; the graft is Man's vanity.'

'In line with your New Church philosophy.'

'Yup. Then I started my own orchard with Isaac Stadden in Licking County. When it was up and running, I wanted to move along. I took a canoe trip down the Licking River to the Muskingum, and then to the Ohio at Marietta. Everywhere I stopped, I planted seeds.'

'We have this enduring image of you strewing seeds as you travelled through Pennsylvania, Illinois, Ohio, Indiana, all kinds of places. It's a beguiling image.'

'But totally hokey! Makes me look like an idiot. Listen, every place I went, I fenced the seedbeds against wildlife, I talked to the local landowners, and I exhorted them to care for the seedlings and to use the fruit wisely. That's good husbandry.'

'I've heard tell that they've made you quite a rich man.'

'Sure. They welcomed me. I planted the seedlings, sold shares in the apples, and came back every couple of years to check up on 'em and collect my earnings. Sell the apples or sell the saplings. It was good old Yankee entrepreneurship.'

'So, your dress and manner doesn't exactly mirror your worldly wealth.'

'I practice what I preach. Simplicity. I've always been generous in sharing all I've got, be it worldly goods, or stories, or books of the New Church. And I know that if I share, others will share. I don't buy clothing; I don't buy food. Hack my hair and beard off myself, unless some kind soul does it for me. Everywhere I go I give and I receive. That's how Our Lord lived His ministry, and we all must strive to regain that.'

'But still, you *are* wealthy.'

'In worldly goods. I've got at least twelve hundred acres

across three states, yet I choose to go around like a vagabond. Look, I'm near 80 years old, and when I'm dead and gone whoever has the acres can keep 'em. I'll get my comforts in the hereafter.'

'I've read of your apple nurseries in so many places, and the history books are filled with the facts of your work, but stories always accumulate and become exaggerated. Legends begin to grow…'

'Yup. The more magazines, church bulletins, newspapers, and what-have-you print the stories, the taller get the tales. That's how I got the moniker, but it suits me. But you've got to be wary of reading too much into Henry Howe's tales. Well meaning. He talked to a lot of people, but he just wrote what they told him: like, I wouldn't kill a mosquito, or I'd douse my campfire in the snow so as not to discommode a bear and her cubs. Don't recall any of that. They'll say anything if it plays in to what they want me to be. So, it's all fine and dandy for you, sitting here yarning with Johnny Appleseed, when there are those who look on me as a living legend!'

'In some ways I believe you are, and now I think you have given me what I came for. Meeting you in person has allowed me to find that deeper truth I alluded to.'

'*No sir*, you have not gotten your deeper truth yet, not by a long way! So, I went all those miles over all those years in any weather, planting all those seeds over hither and yon, and I did all that 'cos people like a nice crunchy apple? That what you think? Hah!'

'Well, yes, selflessly seeding and nurturing apples for the good of many communities…'

'Oh, right! Know what it is about apples grown from seed? You'll mind what Henry David Thoreau said about wild apples? Simply put, you can't eat 'em.'

'Well, then…'

'He said they were "sour enough to set a squirrel's teeth on edge and make a jay scream". So there! Know any chemistry, do you? Listen: sour they may be, but take the sugar in yer apple juice, add a spot of natural yeast, and let it sit. After a week or two you've got alcohol and gas, and that, my friend, is fizzy booze! Whoo-hoo! Why d'ye think I was welcomed far and wide in every home, village, farmstead, church, and cabin the length and breadth of Pennsylvania, Ohio and Indiana?'

At the Guildhall in 1420

It's kind of you to find the time to talk with me, Sir Richard. I'm sure as Lord Mayor of London you must be more than busy!'

'Certainly am, but your request intrigued me. But the way it was worded, I wonder if you have the correct Richard Whittington?'

'What part of the request did you have in mind?'

'Well, the theme of the interview "Rags to Riches" hardly seemed appropriate. I have been blessed with great riches, it is true, but there have been precious few rags in my life.'

'Oh, it's only a metaphor. Surely a rise from base poverty to the most prestigious office in London could be described in that way?'

'It's not a metaphor; it's rubbish.'

'Rubbish? Why rubbish?'

'Because nothing in my life would suggest such a situation.'

'Really? I wonder if we *are* talking at cross purposes then? You did rise from humble beginnings, did you not, and become Lord Mayor of London, not once but three times?'

'Four times. Once appointed, thrice elected. Yes to that, a resounding no to the humble beginnings. We are an ancient family with a seat in Gloucestershire.'

'Oh, really? Well, that's the theme of all the folk stories, legends, poems and plays. Dick Whittington, Lord Ma...'

'Don't you *dare* call me Dick! I am Sir Richard, damn you! And you address me as Your Worship!"

'Oh, dear. I do apologize, Your Worship. But there surely couldn't be two Di... Richard Whittingtons who were Lord Mayor, though.'

'Well, you certainly make it sound as if there were! Kindly explain yourself.'

'The Whittington of which I speak was born in poverty in the Midlands and came south to London to seek his fortune. He was forced to work as a skivvy for a rich merchant named Fitzwarren in Leadenhall Street...

'Never heard of him...'

'Dick—sorry!—had a cat, which he'd bought off an old crone for a penny…'

'I *loathe* cats!'

'And the cat was so good at catching rats that Fitzwarren was impressed. He put the cat aboard one of his trading vessels, where it caught so many rats that a Moorish king paid a fortune in gold for it.'

'This is ridiculous! You're wasting my time.'

'Please, let me continue. Di… this Whittington was so abused in the Fitzwarren household that he fled his servitude and started walking north for home. He'd got as far as Upper Holloway when he heard the bells of St Mary-le-Bow: "Turn again Whittington, Lord Mayor of London". That's what the bells told him.'

'So, you're telling me this buffoon, doubtless with all his meagre belongings in a kerchief tied to a stick, hears bells and turns around? Am I hearing this right?'

'Oh, yes. You see, unbeknownst to him, Fitzwarren's ship had returned with a fortune in gold, the price that had been paid for the cat. When Whittington returned to the house in Leadenhall Street he was rewarded by Fitzwarren because he was the cat's rightful owner. He was now richer than his master and eventually went into partnership with him and married his daughter Alice.'

'And became Lord Mayor of London, I suppose.'

'Exactly. And that's who I was hoping to interview.'

'I have never heard such a parcel of rubbish in my entire life… No, wait! Sit down. We're not finished yet. I was on the verge of having you thrown into the street, but I am more intrigued now than when you first applied to me. Just who are you?'

'I am a scholar of myths, legends and verities.'

'And this… this *Dick* is one of your projects. Is that it?'

'Yes. Where I come from, he has a massive following and a huge public presence. As I said earlier, he is the subject of stories, legends, poems, plays, plaques and sculptures. There's even a Whittington Stone on Highgate Hill at the place where he heard the bells that turned him round.'

'Highgate you say? And this boy is supposed to have walked that far, turned around, and then walked back? And be damned if he'd be able to hear St Mary-le-Bow from that distance anyhow. This is all rubbish!'

'It's as the stories recount, although some say Bunhill. The first instance is in a play called *The History of Richard Whittington, of his lowe byrth, his great fortune* staged in 1604.'

'*Sixteen hundred and four!?* Who *are* you?'

'As I said, a scholar of myths, legends and verities, but not necessarily in the same time and place as your good self.'

'I like to consider myself broadminded, but I'll not be taken for a fool.'

'You may believe me or not as you see fit. I know how to find the door.'

'Stay seated. I will pretend to believe you. Your story is too beguiling to have you dismissed… for now.'

'Your story… er, his story… is recounted in ballads, the earliest of which, from 1605, is lost. We only know its title: *The vertuous Lyfe and memorable death of Sr Ri: Whittington mercer sometymes Lo. Maior of the honorable Citie of London.*'

'Virtuous life you say? That sounds better.'

'Perhaps, except it likely contained all the elements I have already described.'

'What?! The bloody cat, and the bells, and the poverty?'

'Yes, all of it probably. A chapbook of 1656, *The Famous and Remarkable History of Sir Richard Whittington,* has the complete story with embellishments. Over the centuries publications like these and more besides have told the story in many forms.'

'This is monstrous! My life story mocked, my reputation traduced, my very existence the butt of coarse lies. This is character appropriation and assassination on a grand scale. And you tell me people believe these fabrications?'

'The story has been told so often over so many years that it is essentially true by repetition.'

'So there really are people in your world who believe this arrant claptrap?'

'Oh, yes, and much more. I live in a society where truth lies in tatters.'

'Prove it! Prove this calumny or by God, I'll have you trussed up by your thumbs in the Fleet.'

'Well, my favourite source is Wikipedia. Copy and paste, change the wording of course, delete the hyperlinks. I gave a few bucks to them just the other day.'

'!*?#!*...'

'To judge by the whiteness of your knuckles and your choleric countenance, you probably wouldn't appreciate looking at my Samsung tablet just now. I think it's high time I dematerialized...'

S M

Beer and Pasties with King Arthur

Here's a nice shady table. Pull up that chair and let's set the beer jug down here. There's a plate of Cornish pasties coming right up from the bar. I hope you'll like pub food.'

'Hmm, yew tree I see. Sacred sort of tree to sit under, isn't it?'

'I don't think we go for sacred trees much anymore. Now, tell me, sir… er…king… your highness… how should I address you?'

'Just call me Arthur. 'S me name. No need for formality here.'

'Right… Arthur. How's your beer?'

'Never had anything like it. If this is what you get for a brief trip down from the Hallowed Halls, I'm all for it. Aaah…!'

'Good God, you've chugged the whole glass!'

'Top me up, will you? This'll be thirsty work. Who made this stuff?'

'It's Arthur's Ale from Tintagel Brewery, just down the road.'

'Is it, by God? How flattering. It's damned good wallop, let me tell you!'

'Ah, here come our pasties. Thank you. Er, no, I see we won't need knives and forks… Oh, excuse me Arthur, but we don't swig HP Sauce straight from the bottle.'

'Oh, really? Is a bit sharp. Well, so far, the vittles and beer are quite to my liking. So, why am I here? What d'you want to know?'

'Looking at you, your robe is really quite plain for a kingly figure. And sandals, I see.'

'Yeah, the robe's homespun wool, but Guinevere sewed a little fancy stuff on the borders, make me look a little bit more kingly. Important event, this.'

'Funny, I was expecting to meet a… well, a real king, and all that implies.'

'Implies what, exactly?'

'Well, you know, silk and cloth of gold, a bit of bling, some golden torques, or even a crown maybe.'

'Whoa, the stuff you've been reading! Crowns! I suppose you think I've got a magic sword tucked away somewhere?'

'Well, looking at you and thinking of the legends, there is quite the… disparity…'

'Disparity! Hoo, hah! *Whaaarrp!* Excuse my Brythonic! Why don't you order up another jug?'

'More beer coming up.'

'Listen, when the Romans abandoned this island, their rule didn't just collapse. Course it didn't. The sub-kings still had their territory; Vortigern, Ambrosius, all that lot… and me of course. Celtic Christians we were, holding back the invading heathen scum from the Continent. The Matter of Britain. Stuff of legends right there; great foundation to build on. Battles, warfare, prisoners, ransom, quests and gests, love and hate. You have it all.'

'So, I'm in the presence of the actual King Arthur, source of all those great tales!'

'No, no, no! Oh, where can I even begin? Pour me some more beer. Listen: you people always want to chase back to the original, don't you? But no matter how much you dig with your little trowels, and measure it all with your tapes and rulers, you'll never find it. It's gone! You're after something you've invented called "authenticity" but you've no idea what it is! Or how to find it!'

'But we're always seeking the authentic historical verities. That's what research and scholarship and archaeology are all about…'

'Think it is? You're way out of whack. Let me give you an example: this idea of a round table so no knight would be superior to any other? Can you even begin to imagine what pure hogwash that is? Fellow who invented that idea would be the first one thrown to the dogs. But the point is, something so absurdly, fantastically wrong simply has to be true.'

'You're contradicting yourself.'

'No, I'm not. What about the Sword in the Stone, or the

Lady of the Lake, old Merlin, the Holy Grail? Did Joseph of Arimathea *really* bring the Holy Grail to England's pastures green and then hide it somewhere? You tell me.'

'Well, that is one of the least plausible of the myths…'

'Least? Most! And neither was there a sword stuck in a rock. Absolutely, totally nonsensical all of it. But true for all that.'

'I wonder if you're not used to our strong beer…'

'Yes, I—*whaaarrp*—am! Hah, you've got it all round the wrong way. What if what you see here sitting in front of you and quaffing Arthur's Ale is *less* than the reality, not more? What if all that stuff about a round table, a sword in a stone, searching for the Grail, the magical Merlin—the whole great bundle—was more real, more true?'

'You've lost me…'

'Look. What do you know about Tintagel?'

'Well, the legends. Your association with it. Almost an aura, if you like.'

'Really? Well Tintagel, for your information, has actually got precious little to do with me. One tale says that Merlin the Magician disguised my dad Uther to look like Gorlois, king of Cornwall, so he could get into Tintagel Castle and make whoopie with Igraine. Hence me. That's it, end of story. You people love that story so much it's become true!'

'I'm not saying it's *true*, as such.'

'But you're implying it. That's why you chose to meet here. Thousands every year make the same choice; it's practically a pilgrimage site. Listen: you've invoked some sort of spell to bring me to Tintagel and ply me with Cornish pasties and beer, but how do you know you've got the right one?'

'There can only be *one* King Arthur!'

'Rubbish! There's dozens and dozens of 'em: He's in Nennius, the *Annales Cambriae*, Aneirin's *Y Gododdin*, and good old Geoffrey of Monmouth, greatest fabulist of the lot. Then there's Chrétien de Troyes, Thomas Malory… books written in every single period to the present day. The list just goes on and on. You people can't get enough of him.'

'But those are all legends and fables.'

'Damn right they are. I've got 21 direct family members, there are at least 50 other characters in the stories and, of course, there are 24 knights, of which you probably know only a handful.'

'Bedivere, Geraint, Lancelot of course, Galahad…'

'Yeah, the big boys. What about Moriaen or Lamorak or Griflet?'

'Excuse me, but where are we going with this?'

'What I'm saying is that it grows: the fable, the legend. Every one of those retellings needed a new Arthur; and all those characters were needed to secure him in his place. Now, here's this particular one sitting here—homespun HP Sauce swigger and chugger of fine beer—and there's the other versions all rolled together.'

'But one, the original, must be the source of all the others!'

'No-o-o! That's only if you assume we're all one on top of the other, in layers. But we're not; we're alongside.'

'I really can't visualize that…'

'Of course you can't. You searchers after the truth and the original and the authentic think in depths, like strata and archaeology. The deeper you dig, the older it is, right? But myth doesn't work that way.'

'But to all appearances you seem to be the one who lived first. You told me you were a Celtic Christian sub-king, and that was why you were dressed modestly, so I quite naturally assumed that you were the original embodiment.'

'Only if you're thinking vertical, but we all act horizontal.'

'You must be the one! The archetype, the real Arthur!'

'Wrong! Want me to prove it?'

'Go ahead.'

'If I'm this fifth century sub-king fighting it out against the heathen forces of darkness, how could I know about all the other Arthurs? Aneirin, Monmouth, Malory, the whole lot? Only way I could do that is if they were all me. And they are!'

'Then how could you be sitting here in one place in time and space if you're also spread across two millennia of British history?'

'Well, I suppose we couldn't *all* be sitting here, could we? Perhaps even I couldn't...? So, there you sit, alone at a table in this Tintagel pub garden with an empty chair across from you, three drained jugs of Arthur's Ale, a half-finished bottle of HP Sauce, two cleaned plates...'

'And your fading voice. Yes. It's all mythology. And it's all true.'

Canadian Content in the Michigan Forests

'You, sir, are one of America's best-known folk heroes.'

'Me? Thinkin' of somebody else. I'm just a great big hulking lumberjack, moi.'

'But it's not what you are now, it's what you became.'

'Became? You talking nonsense. Who you say you were?'

'It's a bit difficult to describe…'

'Finished me shift, got all night. Sit by the fire, grab a coffee. Eh?'

'I'm a researcher with a particular interest in legends. Judging by your accent you're not from around here. Quebec?'

'So what? Told you, I'm just a lumberjack. Ain't no legends around me.'

'Yes, that's what you are now, but it's not what you'll become. That's why I came to this… ah, neck of the woods. I wanted to tell you your own story.'

'Become? Tell me my own story? So, you talkin' about what ain't happened yet?'

'Right. Would you believe me if I told you I come from a century and a half in the future? I know it's a hard sell.'

'Shit we invent round the campfire, you could tell me you're from the Pope in Rome.'

'I know it's a stretch…'

'Nah. We don't keep dates and times round here. One day just like any other. Can tell you it's 1865; close enough.'

'Well, when I said you were one of America's best-known folk heroes, I meant it. After all, you *are* Paul Bunyan, are you not? I do have the right man.'

'Non, non, *non!* I'm Fournier! Fabian Fournier! Don't know no Paul Bon Jean.'

'Bon Jean, Bunyan. Same name.'

'Where you get that name from? What you wanna know about Paul Bon Jean? He's… he's… he's not real…'

'Really? The Paul Bon Jean I know of was involved in the Papineau Rebellion of 1837, when loggers revolted in St Eustache, Quebec. Huge man, just like you.'

'*Merde!* I know! You're some sort of vigilante come to drag me back. Well, I ain't no Bon Jean, no Bunyan, no nothin'!'

'Sit down; lower your fist. I mean no harm. Honestly. You're safely over the border in another country. Besides, if I really wanted to haul you back to Quebec, do you think I'd sit in conversation with you, drinking this... er... *excellent* coffee? And, what are you, six feet six? Give me a chance in a fist fight, do you?'

'Yeah, I could kill...'

'Yup, and I'm not armed. So, what really happened?'

'Happened?'

'Come on, I'm not some big bad government bogeyman. Like I said, a researcher of legends. So...?'

'Goes no further?'

'You have my word. I am who I say I am. All I want to do is talk.'

'Well then, I ran; up into the north woods after the rebellion. Worked and lived rough, one lumber camp to another. Got into an argument with Fabian Fournier, don't even recall what about. Been drinking. Hit him. I've been roughhousing all my life, but I never hit no one that hard before. He was dead, see? Right out dead, skull busted. One hit. I ran again.'

'A thousand miles to the west.'

'Over time, over time; workin', movin', workin' again.'

'So, you took Fabian Fournier's papers and assumed his identity.'

'Papers? We don't have nothin' doin' with papers! Think I sit around in some parlour drinkin' tea? Papers! Think I can figure out writing, or what?'

'So now, you're not Paul Bon Jean anymore.'

'Well...'

'More to the story than meets the eye?'

'See, we sit around the campfire telling stupid stories. Woodsmen have always done that. They're the lies we like to tell of an evening. I'd tell tales of Bon Jean. See, somebody else, not me. More I told tales, the stupider they got, and the more stupid they got, the less they were about me.'

'Classic deflection! The more stupid they got, the less they were about you.'

'I didn't invent the name Paul Bunyan. I heard that from some guy in Saginaw. Took it off of Bon Jean, I guess. Then everybody was sayin' it. Caught on.'

'Damned right it did. We'd say it'd gone viral. From logging campfires across the whole stretch of the boreal forest, a lust for tall tales throughout the Northern Woods.'

'Yeah, we have lyin' contests; who can spin the best yarn. Biggest lie wins. That's how Bon Jean got to be 12 feet tall, how his voice could split the boughs off of trees.'

'I've read a lot of these. Some people collected them and made books.'

'Books, huh? They come to the right place for tall tales, then. We'd scare the young city guys, telling 'em it was so cold yer curses would hang frozen in midair. How when spring came the curses all thawed out…'

'Yes, and there was a barrage of a winter's worth of filthy language. Heard of the Big Onion River?'

'Oh, yeah. Everybody knows about the Big Onion River. Coldest place in the world; 400 degrees below zero. It's the camp where Bon Jean's giant blue ox lived. Did you know, Bon Jean was the one who cleared the North Dakota forests and dug the hole for Lake Superior? And when he sat down his butt cheeks made Red Lake. His ox trod all the holes that made the lakes of Minnesota, hundreds of them.'

'It's so good to hear all this, coming from the source! Eat your hearts out, folk culture social anthropologists! Having a wonderful time; wish you were here.'

'Yeah, you can laugh. None of that stuff's mine. I hear it comin' back to me. Lies have a way of spreading 'till everyone's telling 'em. Half of the loggers believe Bon Jean was real; some of the old guys even say they've met him, worked on his crew. Now there's competition-winning liars for you! It's all gone flyin' away.'

'Well Fabien, or Bon Jean, or whoever you are, you'll be

pleased to know that the name of Paul Bunyan will live forever. He's in books, newspapers, magazine articles, and brochures. TV, movies, videos, plays, musicals. He appears in commemorative plaques, statues and museum displays from the Atlantic to the Pacific. As I said when we first spoke, you are one of America's best-known folk heroes. And, do you know what's ironic?'

'Ironic? What's ironic mean?'

'It means that a huge lumberjack from St Eustache, Quebec has become an American icon. I can't think of a more grandiose example of national cultural appropriation.'

'I'm just some tree chopper. This is all out of my league. Here, more coffee?'

'Er, no thanks.'

With Bēda at the Abbey of St Paul

'Come in, come in. You are very welcome to the Abbey of St Paul. Have you travelled to Jarrow from far?'

'Um, in a manner of speaking, yes. I am so delighted to meet the Venerable Bede.'

'The name is better pronounced Bēda, which comes from *bēodan*, "to bid or to command", although Heaven knows why; it is the last thing I would be doing. But Venerable, eh? Well, that's nice. I didn't know such an accolade had been bestowed.'

'It hasn't yet, but it will be.'

'Ah… It's going to be *that sort* of conversation, is it? Please take a seat, a glass of wine. And perhaps a little explanation?'

'Thank you. My travelling is more… ah, temporal than geographic.'

'So, I gather. You come from a Northumbria of the future, then, which does not yet exist, to the present, which is all around us. Do I have that right?'

'Yes, but I cannot imagine that you would be so accepting of what should be impossible to you.'

'If I could but discern the ten-thousandth part of the workings of our Father in Heaven, I would consider myself blessed beyond mortals. The impossible is in God's hands.'

'Even so, I travel a great deal in a chronotransitive fashion, but I have never yet had my explanation so easily digested.'

'We see miracles all around us. Let me just say that, had you come to see me earlier you would have found me at Monkwearmouth, but I would have been just a lad. Better to be here and now in Jarrow, so the full gamut of my life's work can be accessible to you. You chose your time well.'

'Yes, I chose this date particularly.'

'You know, then, that in my work *De Temporum Ratione* I dated the years from the birth of our Lord Jesus Christ. So, on that figuring, we are late in the year 734. And that fits with the planning of your, ah… journey?'

'Yes, 734. It's very close to…'

'No, no, no, I'll hear no more, thank you!'

'Forgive me. Perhaps I am presuming too much upon

your credulity? We need not pursue this any further.'

'Oh, far from it! I am sure my faith can withstand such presumption.'

'You're very kind, and amazingly understanding.'

'So, how may I help you?'

'I am a student of Anglo-Saxon poetry…'

'Of what?'

'Um, ah, *present-day* English poetry. The language of the vernacular.'

'Ah, my native tongue and the one we are speaking now. A fine and noble language.'

'I didn't know it was your first language.'

'Oh, yes, I am from these parts and low-born—I have scarcely ever left the precincts of Monkwearmouth/Jarrow—and acquired my Latin, Greek, Hebrew, and other languages much later in life. We have the best library in Britain here at the Abbey of St Paul. Fortunate, then, that you didn't meet the callow youth. I am endeavouring to translate the Gospels into our own tongue so the common people may know the Word. Now, what poetic works in particular did you wish to discuss?'

'In your *Ecclesiatical History of the English People*, you cite what we believe to be the earliest poem in the English language: Cædmon's hymn.'

'Oh, there was a great deal more poetry before that! Do you tell me that none has survived?'

'We know this as the first by a named poet.'

'Oh, that is a sadness. I know from my own poetry, and my work in compiling the *Historia Ecclesiastica*, how much becomes lost to the flail of time. But that is a terrible shame. You know the story of Cædmon's poem, I suppose?'

'Not in as great detail as I might from you directly. Could I presume upon you?'

'Of course you may. Here, drink your wine and I'll pour more. It's poor stuff I'm afraid, but it is expensive to bring better from afar, and it would be such an indulgence. Now,

Cædmon's first work, as you know, is a poem of praise. How well do you know it?'

'I could recite it, if you wish...'

'Oh, please! First in the language you and I are speaking now, and then, if you would be so kind, in your English. It will be of great intellectual stimulation to hear what has become of the language in... what would it be... a millennium and a half?'

'Yes, about that. Well, here goes:

Nu scylun hergan hefaenricaes uard
metudæs maecti end his modgidanc
uerc uuldurfadur swe he uundra gihwaes
eci dryctin or astelidæ
he aerist scop aelda barnum
heben til hrofe haleg scepen.
Tha middungeard moncynnæs uard
eci dryctin æfter tiadæ
firum foldu frea allmectig.'

'Oh, wonderful, wonderful! Bravo! You are a scholar! Now in your own tongue.'

'Well, Bēda, I can't promise you much. Here it is:

Now we must honour the guardian of heaven,
the might of the architect, and his purpose,
the work of the father of glory—as he the beginning of wonders established, the eternal lord,
he first created for the children of men
heaven as a roof, the holy creator
Then the middle earth, the guardian of mankind
the eternal lord, afterwards appointed
the lands for men, the lord almighty.'

'Hardly a blessèd word of it! "Now" at the beginning and "almighty" at the end, and perhaps "heaven" in the middle! How wonderfully our English language has moved along! In the hands of time, it has become quite incomprehensible!'

'I'm pleased that you are amazed. But you were going to

relate Cædmon's story.'

'Just so. Cædmon was a cowherd at Streonæshalch, which is in the precinct of the Abbey of Whitby, at the time of the Abbess Hilda.'

'I know of Whitby from the Great Synod that took place there.'

'Yes, indeed. King Oswiu had called upon the fathers of the church in the year 664 to establish the calculations for the date of Easter. Now, where were we? Ah, Cædmon was a herdsman, not a poet or singer, and one night when the congregation were revelling—singing and playing the harp—he stole away and fell asleep in the byre. He was visited by some person—he was never sure who or what—who asked him to sing about the beginning of all things. He composed the hymn you have just spoken, to both my delight and my bafflement. When he awoke, he approached the chief herdsman who, although sceptical, referred him to Abbess Hilda. When she heard of this, she questioned Cædmon long and hard. Not certain that this rude cowherd might have stolen the hymn from another, she set him the task of writing more along the same lines.'

'So, he wrote more than one work, then?'

'Oh, my goodness, yes. He was from that time forward profoundly gifted. He would take our Gospel texts and make them into verses of great sweetness and poignancy. Hilda declared this vision or dream of his to be a miracle, and brought him into the Abbey where he took monastic vows.'

'We know only of this one…'

'Another sadness. So much is lost while we gain. But if these later words of Cædmon are gone, we may console ourselves that those who heard them gained some solace in the promise of the hereafter that they doubtless contained.'

'True, even though your assertion of their existence would be a terrible teaser to scholars of the future.'

'As to that, I penned some autobiographical notes in the last book of my *Historia Ecclesiastica*, but I think it would be unwise to refer further in writing to this little interview of ours.'

'I suspect your writing might create a dangerous closed causative loop.'

'I beg your pardon?'

'This wine is… quite drinkable.'

Some Words Before the Gallows

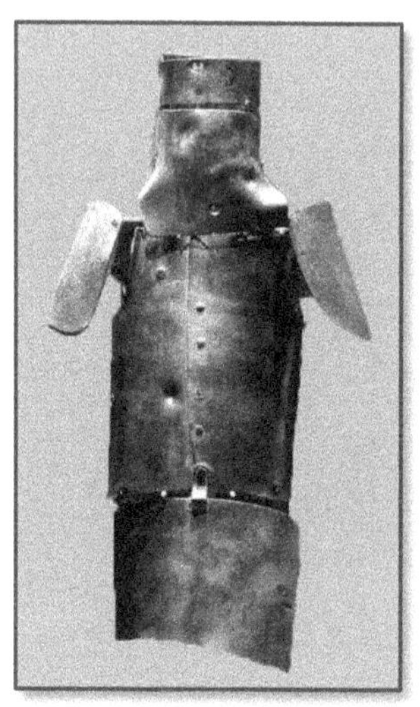

Hello Mr Kelly. I'd like to have a few words with you just an hour before you go to the final punishment for your horrendous reign of terror. Some sentiments of contrition, perhaps.'

'Hey, hey, hey! Not so fast! Talk about prejudgement!'

'Hardly that. Look at the evidence, look at the facts, look at the criminal trial of Ned Kelly and his gang in Melbourne. Open and shut case.'

'You think so, do you? Know what you're missing?'

'I don't think I'm missing anything.'

'To the contrary, my friend. You are only missing the entire socio/cultural context of this series of incidents.'

'How so?'

'If you were to examine and analyse the actions of myself and my associates systematically within a sociological framework, you would be obliged to draw more cogent and, dare I say it, more realistic conclusions.'

'You're not suggesting some extenuating circumstances, are you?'

'I am indeed! Why don't we start with social stigma? Let me count off the points for you: One: I am the son of a criminal who was sentenced to seven years transportation for stealing two pigs; Two: We are of Irish stock and thus lower than dirt; Three: My father died early and left the family penniless; Four: I and my kind are the subjects of systematic discrimination by officers of the government at every level. That do for a start?'

'And this "social stigma" contributes to what, exactly?'

'It's an absolute recipe for a socially engendered societal nonconformity. If a population is both abased and discriminated against by an overarching repressive social construct, it stands to reason that a negative reaction will be the outcome. This is a repeating pattern throughout history, and its results are predictable and inevitable.'

'You speak well and eruditely.'

'That's just you, giving me words. Maybe what you're

writing on that thing of yours is only what I'm thinking?'

'Hmm. So you feel you were treated unfairly?'

'Whatever made you think that? Example: when we were at Eleven Mile Creek in Victoria there was this Chinese pedlar called Ah Fook who claimed I had swung a stick at him and stole 10 shillings because my sister Annie refused him a drink of water. His word, my word. Well, guess who the police would believe?'

'You are saying that they would take the word of a Chinese pedlar over yours?'

'Absolutely they would because we are social pariahs! We're filth. Where a rigid hierarchy of social worth had been established, value judgements are made upon an emotional and not rational basis. Thus, in such a highly class-structured society, assumption of guilt at the lowest echelon is implicit. The police had been dying to lay charges on any of us for years, so guilt was assumed without rational judgement.'

'So, you were arrested?'

'Oh, yeah. Charged with highway robbery. Said I'd claimed to be a bushranger. They held me in a cell for ten days on remand.'

'And then…?'

'Even police require proof, but enough family members gave me the word that they had to dismiss the charges. And there was huge sympathy in the neighbourhood. But, of course, dismissal of charges isn't a declaration of innocence, is it? I had a target on my back from then on.'

'So, they were watching you for any sign of further deviant behaviour?'

'Oh, yes. Like whistling kites, they were. If anything, their failure to indict paradoxically potentiated my guilt in their eyes. In their non-rational evaluation, guilt was implicit. They felt thwarted because they had been working unknowingly within a flawed class structure construct.'

'How flawed, exactly?'

'Where the structure of a given society entertains the

very concept of a criminal class, there is always going to be a corresponding assumption of inherent criminality.'

'Assumed to be guilty, then?'

'Exactly. *Habeas corpus* turned on its head. Look, when my pa finished his seven years transportation sentence do you think he was automatically an innocent man? Oh, sure! Doesn't work that way; once a crook always a crook. The whole Kelly family became victims of police persecution. Shit, what am I saying? The whole neighbourhood. The whole damned district!'

'And the police pulled you in again fairly soon after your first charge was dismissed?'

'Yeah. I was accused of rustling cattle and they threw me in jail. I'd been hanging around with Harry Power, a bush-ranger who was always moving horses and cattle in ways the authorities didn't like. He had a flexible understanding of property.'

'But you were innocent?'

'There was no clear evidence I wasn't. Seven weeks inside, then charge dismissed. Then six months... can't remember what they said I'd done... ah, it all gets to be a blur. I know I was more inside than out for years.'

'But surely, with all these strings of convictions, there must have been some substance.'

'Look it's self-fulfilling isn't it? Where we lived all of us were in it—brothers, cousins, in-laws, the lot. It was a way of life. But the point is, we didn't choose it. I think there is an excellent argument to be made for a paradigm wherein the criminal is cast in the role of the unwitting victim of social circumstances entirely beyond his control.'

'So, it's a political issue?'

'It's a class issue. As long as we're living in a rigid social caste system, with limited or non-existent vertical mobility, there will always be disadvantaged populations at the lower end living outside the laws of the comfortable majority.'

'You mean criminals?'

'Of course I mean criminals! You know what we are; I'm just telling you how we got here.'

'Well, rustling and horse napping are one thing, but then it began to get ugly, didn't it? There was the arrest warrant for your brother Dan.'

'They came to Ma's place in Eleven Mile Creek. Arsehole cop called Fitzpatrick and some other uniformed criminals. Bowls right in without any paperwork and the next thing you know he says he's been shot. Never a wound on him! And here's where the fix is in: three cops swore that I had shot him, and that I had confessed to it! *Me, confess!* So, who do *you* believe? I wasn't even there, but three upstanding officers against one felon said I was. That's how they operate.'

'Things began to escalate…'

'Well, things would, wouldn't they? They ran in Ma, her son-in-law William, and the neighbour, charged with aiding and abetting. Me and Dan had £100.00 on our heads, so we took off into the Wombat Ranges. Joe Byrne and Steve Hart came in later. Four of us holed up against the whole corrupt system of so-called justice.'

'I read that Mrs Kelly went down for three years, and the two guys got ten each.'

'And wouldn't that tip anyone over the edge? Three years for an old lady who was in the house, ten for a witness, and ten for a neighbour. What had they done to deserve anything like that? Bastard of a judge was purely vindictive. Sir Somebody-or-other. When we heard that, we knew it was us or them.'

'And the resulting mayhem—shootings, hostages, fires, bank robberies—is, of course, world famous.'

'Yeah, and what should be world famous is the letter I dictated to Joe Byrne in Jerilderie. I told the whole story: the police corruption, the persecution, the framing, the faked-up evidence, the so-called witnesses… Know what happened? Nothing. Too scared to let out the voice of the lowest level of society. Corrupt from top to bottom.'

'I know what you wrote.'

'*What?!* How could you? They buried it.'

'It's lost, but long after your death a clerk in the Crown Law department copied it. The copy exists to this day.'

'This day? What day? After my *death?*'

'I wasn't honest with you at the opening of this interview because I wished to draw you out. I'm from a century in the future.'

'Oh, right! As big a liar as a policeman!'

'What reason would I have to lie to a man who is condemned to hang in less than an hour, and what reason would you have to disbelieve me?'

'Well...'

'Want me to prove it? I found one piece of the letter so amusing and... honestly expressed, that I can quote you word for word. Remember what you said about the Victorian police? "A parcel of big ugly fat-necked wombat headed big bellied magpie legged narrow hipped splaw-footed sons of Irish Bailiffs or English landlords". All comes back?'

'That's... that's what I wrote...'

'And "This cannot be called wilful murder for I was compelled to shoot them, or lie down and let them shoot me". Same letter.'

'I don't know who you are or what you are, but you know stuff that can't be known.'

'There was a lot of sympathy for you and your gang among the folks of northern Victoria, wasn't there?'

'Anybody oppressed by their system; not just Irish bog-trotting scum. Anybody, anywhere would come round and see firsthand how the system creates criminals.'

'Well, it also creates heroes. Go to the gallows with this in mind: Ned Kelly, a man who rebelled against an oppressive and corrupt system, stood tall in Glenrowan, Victoria clad in metal armour like a white knight of old. His legend lives on in poems, images, stories, songs and stage.'

'Ah well, I suppose it has come to this.'

A Brown Ale in Ely

I've always enjoyed visiting the Fens, so it was appropriate to ask you to come to Ely so we could have this little conversation. It's been half an hour since I called you up, and you've finished your ale. Are you ready?'

'Ready…? What… It's all changed since I lived here. The monastery has become a cathedral, and you've drained the Fens. And all this… bustle!'

'Yes, a lot has happened in over a millennium. Are you comfortable to continue? I know it's always a shock.'

'A thousand years? If you believe in an afterlife as strongly as I do, it comes easier. But why am I brought to this strange place? What do you want?'

'Merely to ask a few questions. As I said, are you comfortable with this?'

'Ask then. Pour me some more of this excellent ale.'

'Here. It's Ely brown ale from the Forehill Brewery. So, tell me, why the appellation "Hereward the Wake"?'

'Wake is from the Anglo-Saxon word *wæcnan*, which means "watchful", but more to the point, Hereward is not my real name.'

'Really? That's how you are known.'

'Known? Am I really? The name's from *here*, which means "army or host", and *ward*, which is one who takes care. It was given to me by my men. My real name's Asketil—a family name—but you won't find that written anywhere. As if any parent would call a child Watchful Commander!'

'You have Danish connections?'

'There was lots of Danish blood since away back. All the east coast, the Danelaw. My grandfather was Danish, father and mother good old Anglo-Saxon, as you would say.'

'So, you were Watchful Commander to your men?'

'About right. That's what I was, that's what I did, and that's what they called me. Hereward the Wake.'

'But let's not get ahead of ourselves. How did you come to be the watchful commander of men, the rebel we know about? It was after the Norman invasion of 1066, correct?'

'Yes, but go back further. We had land in Bourne, near Peterborough, where I grew up. I admit I was a handful for my father and it got to the point where he didn't want me around. People would expel wayward sons, and so I was exiled at the age of eighteen. Spent years fighting in Flanders as a mercenary with Robert the Frisian, part of Baldwin V's land grab.'

'So that was before the Normans?'

'Yes, years before. Then when I got back from Flanders in 1067, the year after the invasion, I found our land had been confiscated by this Norman bastard, Ivo de Taillebois, and my father and brother murdered.'

'I've read terrible things…'

'Oh, yes. You find your brother's head stuck on a stake on what used to be your home, you tend to want revenge. And while I was outside the house, I could hear the bastards celebrating! A whole bunch of drunken Norman soldiers insulting us local Anglo-Saxons. Got together a couple of stalwart lads…'

'Yes…?'

'The Normans were so pissed they couldn't see straight. Me and two others, we slaughtered 15 of them while they tripped over each other, fumbled for their swords, or fell into the fire. And then, by God, we lopped off their heads—all 15 of 'em—and stuck 'em on stakes where my brother had been. Had to forage around in a copse to find enough wood. That's the only sort of message these Norman scum understand.'

'Then it was time to "leave" the neighbourhood, I would guess.'

'Damned right it was! We gathered up a band of followers and headed for safety in Peterborough Abbey. My uncle, Abbot Brand, a good Danish sympathiser, was in charge there so we were safe… for the time being. He knighted me right there—abbots could do that—then we took horse to Lowestoft, and ship to Flanders.'

'I understand you had an issue with William de Warenne,

who was the Norman power in East Anglia at this time.'

'He had land all over the place, stolen after the invasion. The king rewarded him richly after he had stood by him at Hastings, giving away what wasn't his right, left and centre. De Warenne's brother-in-law Frederick got in my way when I was in Flanders; we had a little argument, drew swords, and he ended up without a heartbeat. Of course, after that de Warenne had a hate on for me.'

'What did you do in Flanders?'

'Plan, plan, plan. Word was that an army of warriors had been sent from Denmark by Sweyn II Estrithson, so I returned, rallied around as many men as I could, and marched for the Isle of Ely where they had their base. Then I learned that my uncle Abbot Brand had been ousted from Peterborough Abbey, replaced by this turd Turold de Fecamp, a greedy Norman swine who was using feoffments to line his pockets, and those of his friends. In his hands, feoffment was a kind of legalized theft: transferring land and selling it for cash.'

'As you mentioned earlier, at that time Ely was an island in the Fens.'

'And we knew the ways through the marshes like no foreign usurper could. We marched from the Isle of Ely and attacked Peterborough Abbey. The whole parcel of them ran away—turd Turold, monks, laymen, everyone. We sacked the whole place and liberated the church treasures.'

'When you say "liberated", one of the sources I read said that you wished to preserve Ango-Saxon treasures from Norman possession. You were vouchsafed a vision of St Peter.'

'Hah! Believe that one if you like; makes me look better. Sweyn's lot kept the loot; no idea what happened to it. Then we retreated with the swag to Ely.'

'I read that Earl Morcar of Northumbria became involved.'

'Just like me, he'd been kicked out by the Norman scum—dispossessed as I'm sure you would say—so he marched south to join us. Small army, but men-et-arms nonetheless.

Our scouts led them through the marshes; it was treacherous country unless you knew the way.'

'Once your rebel army...'

'Liberation army!'

'Sorry... *liberation* army... was encamped on the Isle of Ely, the Normans really began to take notice.'

'Oh, yes! If you deprive 15 Normans of their heads and stick them on poles, sack a cathedral and make off with the treasures, and then consort with foreigners on English soil, you're likely to stir up a wasp's nest. The self-styled King William was... unhappy.'

'But you couldn't win, could you? Not against the might of a conquering army.'

'Never hoped we could. It was red, impulsive vengeance, but once you've started something like that you can't just stop. "Ooh, sorry, didn't mean it. Now, where were we?" Still, there were other insurrections throughout the country, so you look at your chances. It may look different now. But, yes, we were isolated on our island.'

'And that proved a challenge for the Norman army.'

'And a source of rich amusement.'

'How so?'

'You have never seen such a botched-up mess as their attempt to cross the marshes. See, there was this huge army on dryland atop a hill, off in the direction of London, with Aldreth's Causeway between them and us. It's deep, marshy land, lots of standing water. So, they built this great wooden pathway right across the water; a mile long, it was. We were concerned at first; finish that bridge and we were outnumbered and done with. Then, with most of their horsemen halfway across we could see what would happen. Sure enough, the whole structure tipped up. Scores of them, maybe hundreds, struggling in the water, horses, armour and weapons. We stood on the other side and roared with laughter, shouting insults, as they drowned in droves in a few feet of water.'

'I read that you disguised yourself as a potter to spy on the king.'

'Rubbish. Spying on what king? Bastard was in London. And what information could we possibly want that we didn't have already? We were safe enough on the Isle of Ely.'

'Then there's the story of a witch who cursed you until you set fire to a tower she was in.'

'Who thinks up this stuff? But we were ready for them when they tried a second time. We set fire to the reeds so they were between fire and water, then rained arrows down on them.'

'I know how it ended, but you tell me.'

'Betrayal. Christian betrayal. Abbot Thurstan of Ely Abbey didn't like a whole army billeted on his house, and he must have been fearful of retribution should he succour us. So, the swine took 30 pieces of silver to sell us to some Norman bastard called Hugo Belsar. He showed him the way through the fens.'

'But, in defence of Thurstan, you had sacked Peterborough Abbey…'

'That's a viewpoint, certainly. Anyhow, we were overrun.'

'Not the end for you, though.'

'No. Morcar was taken and imprisoned—don't know what became of him—but I escaped across the marshes with a few of my men. We knew the ways.'

'One story has it that you parlayed with King William, who pardoned you and allowed you to remain peacefully in East Anglia.'

'*Who thinks up this stuff?* My God! Can you imagine this cold, ruthless bastard on a campaign of expunging all resistance throughout his entire stolen kingdom, suddenly turning around and just *being nice?* I've never heard anything so stupid!'

'So, what did you do?'

'I skulked around the Fens for years with a few stalwarts, living off whatever sympathisers could safely give us, and murdering Normans when we could. I took a shot at that bastard de Warenne and knocked him off his horse, but he lived, Satan roast him. Eventually, I took ship to Flanders. That's where I died… until I appeared here, that is!'

'Do you know of a man named Leofric the Deacon?'

'*Leofric?* How could you know of him? *How?*'

'He wrote a book, now lost, of all your exploits. It became damaged, with parts missing, then translated from Anglo-Saxon into Latin and much… improved. Over the centuries scholars take original works and embellish them, adding material either from found history or from imagination. This one's called the *Gesta Herewardi,* and that's the main source of my information about you.'

'Leofric… Leofric was my companion for years; confessor, friend, fellow fighter. I'm overwhelmed.'

'Well, the *Gesta Herewardi* makes you out to be an Anglo-Saxon hero, resisting the Norman occupation, and striking at the forces of subjugation and servility. Leofric said you were driven by honesty, chivalry in warfare, and valiant support for the common man.'

'Ah, Leofric, you damned flatterer! Was he the one who thought up that stuff? The old liar!'

'Perhaps, but much of it might be a later attempt to create a legend, taking Leofric's original and embellishing it. So, here's my dilemma: there are heroes throughout the ages whose names echo down the millennia. Whose exploits are polished, magnified and made the subject of legend. You, of all people, would fit into that mould. A freedom fighter against tyranny on a par with the greatest of heroes of myth and legend. And yet…'

'And yet?'

'And yet, who knows of you? Sure, I do because I make characters such as yourself my special area of study. But the average person in the street? Hereward the *who?*'

'I'm glad at least that you know my story, and that something was written in a book. And that Leofric, my companion for years, lives in memory. I'll tell you something else: this brown ale makes my journey to this Ely well worthwhile.'

'Have another glass. And I promise you, I'll do my best by you. That's why you're here and that's why I'm hearing your story.'

'Here's beer and good company! *Gōd hælð!*'

The Newgate Hornpipe

Welcome to Newgate—I think not!'

'I don't know if I've visited a more noisome pit of hell in all my temporal travels.'

'Well, hold your damned nose then. A most salubrious final residence for one so falsely accused. What d'ye, say?'

'You are the notorious pirate Captain William Kidd, are you not?'

'William Kidd yes, pirate no! So, you've been inveigled by the lies and deceit as well. And who in hell are you anyway?'

'I'm just one who wishes to have a talk with you before your appointment with the gibbet.'

'There's nothing you can do for me. They even withheld the money to buy me legal counsel, the conniving sons of whores.'

'Are you able to tell me how you came to be here?'

'Aye, why not tell all before I dance the Newgate hornpipe on a rope of my enemies' weaving?'

'Perhaps your version of things will help separate the wheat from the chaff, as it were. As to the notoriety of piracy, how do you plead?'

'Don't play the lawyer with me! Plead my arse, when I'm within half an hour of the long drop. I am not a pirate and you clearly know nothing of privateering.'

'Well, I do understand that you were commissioned by the Crown to protect English interests throughout the Caribbean, the east coast of America, and as far as the Indies. And I do know that the privateer would be sanctioned by Letter of Marque, whereas the pirate operated outside the law.'

'Ah, sea lawyer, are you? Smart, you are. So, tell me then, what happens when some swine changes the rules?'

'Such as?'

'In 1695, I got a Letter of Marque from Richard Coote, the Earl of Bellomont, may Satan piss into his open mouth for eternity. He was the Governor of New York, Massachusetts Bay, and New Hampshire, not that he ever graced anywhere but New York city with his vile presence. I was to hunt down French ships wherever I found 'em, confiscate their cargoes, and go after pirates like Maze, Tew and Wake.'

'True pirates then, as you were not?'

'Right! Scum of the seas they were. We set sail on the *Adventure Galley*, financed by a whole parcel of landed gentry, including King William III himself. That's how damned legitimate our enterprise was. Then comes the *Quedagh Merchant*, a 400 tonner off the coast of Chennai. Hell of a prize, but that's when gold turned to pig shit.'

'I recall reading that you overhauled her in the Indian Ocean and hoisted a French flag.'

'Aye, standard practice. Lure the bastards with subterfuge then break out the English colours. A sovereign ruse.'

'So, what went amiss?'

'Well, here's the mess: she was Hindoostan-owned, flying the colours of Armenia, with a mostly Hindoo crew; she was captained by an Englishman, there was a frog second-in-command, and an agent for the East India Company had brokered the voyage. But the thing is, she had been promised safe passage by the French, so the froggy connection made the capture legal, at least in my eyes. It was only later when we started divvying up the spoils that I found some of the cargo was owned by this Muklis Khan, who was a good friend of the Grand Moghul of Hindoostan.'

'So, there was a diplomatic shit storm in London?'

'Shit storm? Nice turn o' phrase you have. That's good! Aye, the greedy bastards who had commissioned me got cold feet, and turned around and declared this as piracy.'

'Was there not an Act of Grace; in effect, a royal pardon for pirates operating in the Indian Ocean?'

'Yes, but no. See, I was exempted because my name was associated with Whig politicians in England. Get close to scum, you get infected. And I only discovered that when I got to Anguilla, in the Caribbean. So, we dumped the ship, converted some of the loot to specie, and made for Boston with the rest. I was under summons, see, but I still thought that when it came down to it, Bellomont would see me through.'

'Speaking of a nice turn of phrase, I recall your hopes regarding Bellomont and Satan's eternal urination.'

'Hah! The turncoat swine had me arrested and tried, found guilty, and sent across the Atlantic in chains.'

'And here you are in Newgate. But, weren't you carrying the treasure to Boston, ostensibly to give to Bellomont?'

'Yes! That was my trump card, or so I thought. I was sure that the treasure would be sufficient to have the swine take my side but, just in case, I buried it on Gardiner's Island in Long Island Sound.'

'Ah, yes, now we hit the treasure trove! You are mostly known to us as a secreter of buried treasure, of course.'

'Known to you? Who are you anyway?'

'Nobody of any consequence at this late stage. But, the buried treasure…'

'Never did it but the once, and it wasn't secret. Hardly even buried. I told Gardiner and his wife where it was—stuck in a cleft in a ravine between Bostwick's Point and their house —and told 'em it was for the Governor of the Massachusetts Bay Colony, and to look after it. Christ, I even gave his wife some of the Grand Moghul's cloth of gold.'

'What did the treasure consist of?'

'Oh… A box of gold, two boxes of silver, a chest. I mind there were Spanish dollars, rubies, diamonds, candlesticks, things of that sort.'

'So, that hoard wasn't lost, then? Buried with no known location?'

'No, I told you! Course it wasn't! What's the point of burying stuff if nobody knows where it is? That Judas Bellomont tried to screw the location out of me. Gave up, but in the end, he found out where it was and ordered Gardiner to deliver it as "evidence". Evidence my arse!'

'So, you say that Gardiner's Island was the only time you ever concealed treasure?'

'If you can say "concealed" with a straight face when everybody knew where it was, then yes. What is this inquisition?'

'Did you not visit Oak Island at some time in your career?'

'Oak Island? Oak Island where?'

'Off the coast of Nova Scotia.'

'Never heard of it. Was in Halifax once. Why?'

'There is a legend that you had buried a vast treasure at the bottom of a pit, with channels from the sea devised to drown unwary diggers.'

'Why in Christ's name would I do that? Why would anybody bury treasure? Makes no sense.'

'Perhaps if you feared capture you would attempt to hide it away?'

'No, you wouldn't. Christ! You'd make all sail for the nearest safe port where you knew you could find a fence who asks no questions. They're worldwide. Cochin, Kalliguilon, Anguilla… Buried treasure, my arse!'

'Thing is, in my, er… time… a vast literature based on sunken chests, treasure maps, and swashbuckling maritime exploits has been spawned. You know, walking the plank, peglegs, cryptic charts, the jolly roger, ciphers… It's quite an industry.'

'This "time" of yours sounds as if it ought to be consigned lock, stock and barrel to Bedlam. That's where this Oak Island nonsense came from, eh?'

'Well, yes. Rumours spread that a treasure connected to you was buried there, and hundreds of hours and huge amounts of money have been spent over two centuries of excavation. It's become known as "the money pit"… What's so amusing? For one destined for the gallows, you can still roar with laughter?'

'Money pit! Oh, that is *so* rich! Money pit!'

'Well, I'm pleased that this little visit has lightened your spirit.'

'Aye, belike I'll die with a smile on my lips. *Money pit!*

The Pied Piper Tells All

The year 1248 is a very specific date for an action with so few clear explanations. It can't be just a fairy tale, can it?'

'And you've even got the day: 26th June of that year. Very specific indeed. So, that's why you conjured me back here to Hameln, eh? Want a definitive answer right from the piper's mouth? What *did* happen to those 130 children?'

'Well, yes. That's the objective of my temporal quests; to interview the protagonists face-to-face and maybe get solid answers.'

'Hmm... Solid answers... We'll see... So many explanations, so few answers, eh?'

'Just so.'

'The story—my story—is, at present, a profound mystery. Your first task, I feel, is to ascertain exactly who it is that you have plumped down here at a café in the *Hauptmarkt* of 21st century Hameln. After all, as it's the very date of the abduction, Hameln is overwhelmed with celebrating look-alikes.'

'Yes, and don't you blend in well? They're all masquerading as you, but as in all my other interviews, I know I am speaking with the very man. To wit, the Pied Piper of Hameln himself.'

'You mean the psychopathic serial pederast who made off with the kids for his own vile purposes?'

'That is one of the more prurient theories. Do you deny it?'

'Ah. Before I answer that, let me turn the tables on you. Instead of me telling you who I really am, why don't you tell me what the 21st century thinks of me? What theories, conjectures, suppositions and plain guesses have the scholars of your time, and those of intervening years, hazarded as to my identity? And while you're about it, order some more coffee, will you. This is strange stuff but quite palatable.'

'All right. If you want to keep your cards close to your chest, I'll open first. The long-standing fairy tale is that Hameln was afflicted with a plague of rats, so the burghers took you at your promise to rid the town of the vermin.'

'Go on.'

'After you had piped all the rats away, the town council refused to pay you, so you played your pipe again and the town's children followed you into oblivion. You were an evil enchanter.'

'I see. Well, in this scenario of yours the rats do complicate matters.'

'How so?'

'Simply that they never existed.'

'There were no rats in Hameln?'

'No, no, no! Every habitation in Christendom and beyond had rats; they were part of life in filth-ridden villages, towns and cities. Infesting the middens and brazenly coming forth into the streets and houses.'

'So, you say you had no role as an exterminator?'

'Think about it for more than just a couple of seconds. Have you ever heard of any creature, anywhere, at any time, being attracted to the sound of any musical instrument, let alone following in droves? I say attracted; creatures are oft repelled. It's beyond naïve. It's bloody ridiculous.'

'So, no rats?'

'No rats.'

'Hmm, no mesmerising rat/child-catcher either, then?'

'No. And it's not a matter of beliefs at the time; it's a matter of pragmatic fact. Couldn't happen then, but could, of course, be concocted later.'

'Well, it's only a fairy tale anyway.'

'It is now.'

'So, we can set that one aside then. Ah, here's our coffee… Thank you. So, set aside the fairy tale…'

'Yes, we can indeed. Next?'

'The loss of the children could be assigned to natural causes. Until the modern era there were many childhood diseases, some of which were highly contagious. The fact that 130 children could contract such a disease is not beyond probability.'

'And the date? Specific to the very day?'

'June 26th could have been the date that the town council or the church authorities set aside for a memorial service, presumably after the illness had abated and the deaths had ceased.'

'Plausible, at least. Try me with some more guesses.'

'Theories, please. There was the possibility of the Pied Piper leading the children away on a Children's Crusade.'

'Ah yes, conflated tales of two visionaries—Nicholas, a Rhineland shepherd, and Etienne a French shepherd boy—who led children in a campaign to free the Holy Land from the Infidel. The so-called "children" were, in fact, poor wandering peasants, displaced and hopeless. It was a time of terrible upheavals: wars, plagues, pestilences. The church referred to these people collectively as children, but they were of all ages.'

'So, it is unlikely that a similar visionary would have come along a generation later and lured people away on a holy quest?'

'Well, certainly not to take them south over the Alps and then take ship for Outremer. Not guilty!'

'Well, there's a theory that the 26th of June is the date of pagan midsummer celebrations. It's said that the children followed the Piper to the Koppen, which is usually translated as "hills". They lit fires on the hills during their rites, while the Pied Piper, a pagan shaman, led them up to the ceremonies, and thus to their slaughter.'

'Laughable. The 26th of June was nowhere near the date of the solstice that year. The solstice was on Sunday 14th of June, almost two weeks out. Wrong!'

'Then there's an even more fanciful suggestion that the children were afflicted with St Vitus' Dance, a mass psychogenic illness. There were many cases in the Middle Ages of whole populations being afflicted with manic dancing, and there's a contemporary account from Erfurt, where a group of youths danced out of town, wildly gyrating, and ending up exhausted many miles away.'

'And this "illness" of yours has been assigned to the Hameln incident of 1248?'

'It has.'

'I like the sound of that one best. You've got the musical aspect of the dance, the lure of the pipe, and the historical incidence of manic dancing. The hole in the theory is, according to the Hameln legend, it was only children that were affected, yet the contemporary records show people of all ages being caught up in this mass hysteria. A sort of medieval flash mob, as I think you would describe it?'

'So, you're not really convinced?'

'There's also the fact that they didn't come back once the music stopped. They could hardly have melted into thin air with their exertion. Awkward, that.'

'Yes, some prom, that was. That *is* a hole in the argument, certainly. So, not a front-runner?'

'Hmm… I'd give it a five out of ten, I think. What else do you have?'

'Well, the Pied Piper could have been a *lokator,* many of whom roamed the area of Hameln. They were agents during the *Ostseilung,* the mass migration of German-speaking people to the east and north. The nobles and church elders in such locations as Pomerania and Brandenburg sent recruitment officers to Lower Saxony, Westphalia and further west and south. They would arrive in market places or town squares, gaudily dressed and often heralded by a trumpet or a fife, and coerce citizens, mostly the young and the energetic, recruiting them with promises of better lands.'

'Oh, you *have* been doing your reading!'

'It's easy these days. It's all on the Web. Can't remember the last time I cracked a book.'

'So, then, why would these nobles and church elders lure people to their lands? Were there not enough peasants in their demesnes already? A leading question, my friend.'

'After the defeat of the Danes in 1227 at the Battle of Bornhöved, the indigenous Slavs south of the Baltic were driven out, and land became available for settlers. It has been noticed that place names in these more northern and eastern locations are in many cases identical to those from which the settlers left.

Westphalian place names are found in the northeast, like the five Hindenburgs and three Spiegelbergs, and there's a close relationship between Beverungen south of Hameln and Beveringen northwest of Berlin. There's even a Beweringen in what is now Poland.'

'And family names?'

'Oh, yes, Hamel, Hamler and Hamelnikow for example.'

'All of which leads your scholars to the conclusion that I was ah… instrumental… in a mass migration. There are just two more hoops to jump through: to wit, the fact of "children" and the fact of an exact date.'

'As to "children", as you said earlier, people were referred to collectively as children, even though they were of all ages. Examine the Latin word *pueros* in the extant documents.'

'Exactly, my friend. Had your theorists not heard of the Children of Israel? It's a bloody literary device in many languages, that's all! So, to the date, then.'

'Now we're right down to the crunch! You, sir, appeared in the town square of Hameln that day in all your regalia, tootling your silver fife, and the poor, the disaffected, the displaced, gathered round and listened to your spiel.'

'Yes and no. Yes, it was Friday the 26th of June and the weekly market was in full swing. It wasn't a fife, though. Nobody plays a fife to attract attention in a busy market. It was a silver trumpet three feet long carrying the red and gold banner of Konrad II von Salzwedel of Gützkow. What you have wrong is this idea of the poor, disaffected, displaced. Not so. The ones who gathered around me and my scrivener that day were ordinary townsfolk who were sick and tired of excessive taxation, furious with a venial and uncaring town council, overwhelmed with stink and rubbish—the tale of the rats might possibly stem from that—and ready to sell-up and move on. I came at exactly the right time because they were ready to revolt. That day in the market square I offered them a golden exit strategy.'

'How much did you offer?'

'Nothing. Nothing but a piece of paper. Never give anybody anything except promises, otherwise they will take the money and run. I had land allotments on paper and all we needed to do was to apply their name, and have them sign or mark. We ran out of deeds, so keen were those people to wipe Hameln off their boots. I'm sure we only brought about 50 deeds, though.'

'So, this was an exodus of talented people? Numbers exaggerated perhaps?'

'Oh, yes. Woodworkers, cobblers, smiths, tradesmen; all young, energetic folk and their families, citizens the town could ill afford to lose.'

'Now I get a glimmering of how the Pied Piper legend arose.'

'Yes, a town council with something embarrassing to hide: "Why did so many of your best and most productive citizens leave at that time?" "Because we were so venial and corrupt, we forced them to join the *Ostseilung*". "Oops, sorry. I mean they were... er... spirited away by a demon piper. Yes, that's it, a demon piper. Pied, he was". True in essence, suitably plausible for later historical interrogation, and rife for romantic interpolation. I am the legend; just delete the rats, please.'

'So, no psychopathic serial pederast, then?'

'Sorry to disappoint.'

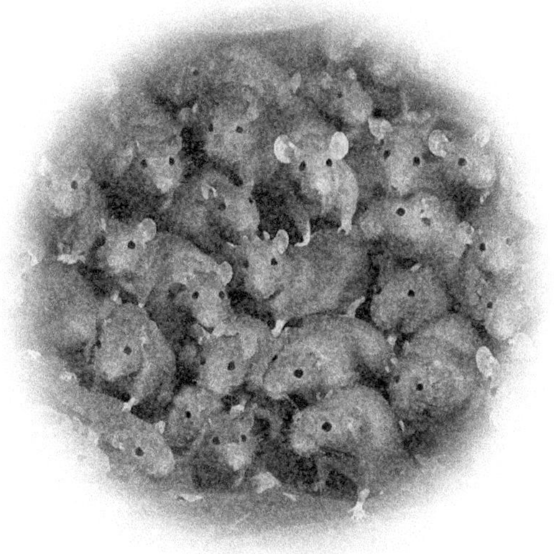

Bonfire Night

'Welcome to the 20th century Mr Fawkes. I hope I haven't disturbed you.'

'I was on the scaffold... I jumped... Am I in hellfire? What's that terrible blaze?'

'Don't worry, that's just our Guy Fawkes Night bonfire. We'll be setting off the fireworks as soon as it's fully dark.'

'Fireworks?'

'Yes, we've burnt you in effigy already, so now it's time to celebrate your plot with gunpowder.'

'My plot... Gunpowder... *How many* centuries...?'

'Three and a half, such is your fame. It is the year 1956.'

'You tell me it is three centuries and a half forward, and I am *here!* Why am I here?'

'I brought you here. I hope you don't mind. I have this uncanny ability of fishing in the past and bringing people forth to this century. I went back sixty-five years myself, to my own childhood. I've so wanted to talk to you.'

'Oh, 'tis a dream, and a solid one. I'll play along as it seems I must. Better than the fires of hell, at any rate.'

'Good. Enjoy the warmth of the fire. Here's some hot cocoa and some roasted chestnuts. Now, tell me, your story has been told over and over again down the centuries, and we celebrate it to this day on November 5th, but you never put a word to paper yourself, did you?'

'I didn't write; I *acted*.'

'Yes, and I suppose putting details of your plotting down on paper might not have been wise.'

'Oh, true indeed. You have a rapier understanding. Let me see: should the authorities have intercepted communications to the effect that James Stuart, the Protestant spawn of Satan, was to be blown sky-high with gunpowder, things might have gone ill with me. That about sums it up, I think.'

'Quite.'

'As it was, 'twas another sealed the fate of the enterprise. Caught with me hose down.'

'Exactly, we know how you were surprised in the act,

but I would love to hear the back story. How it all came to this.'

'You know, of course, under the tyrant Elizabeth, the Anglican Church held sway in England. I was born in the north, in York, and when I was eight years old my father died. My mother soon remarried a recusant Catholic and I was converted to Catholicism at a tender age.'

'What is a recusant?'

'Recusants were those who refused to attend Anglican services, because we knew in our hearts that their false rites would lead only to damnation. We were subject to fines, property confiscation and imprisonment. All our worship was conducted in secret.'

'Yes, England remained staunchly Protestant under King James I, the Stuart who had succeeded Elizabeth.'

'Ill-tempered Scottish yokel! The oaf scarcely spoke English. Hundreds, thousands fled the country rather than sneaking and burrowing. Hiding our books, hiding the instruments of the holy mass, always looking over the shoulder. It was intolerable. When I was in my 20s, I took ship to the Netherlands.'

'Why the Low Countries?'

'I wished to join the fight with the Catholic Spanish against the Dutch Revolt. The Protestant Hapsburgs sought to wrest the Spanish Crown from its dominion over the Netherlands. I would fight for any cause, anywhere, whose end was to establish the true Catholic religion.'

'Did you not approach the Spanish Crown for the support of a Catholic rebellion in England?'

'I did, but I got nowhere. Spain had burned its bridges with the Armada in 1588 and it was damned if it would drop its britches again. Besides, it was near bankrupt with warfare. England could fend for itself and be damned to it.'

'It was while on the Continent you met Thomas Wintour.'

'Wintour, Winter, yes. We were on a similar errand, with equally fruitless ends. I went back to England with him early in 1605 because we had heard interesting news about a possible plot against the upstart Stuart. Damn me, this cocoa stuff is delicious!'

'Have a top-up. Hold your cup under the Thermos. There... And that's when you met Robert Catesby?'

'Yes, and the others. There was Wintour's brother Robert, Christopher and John Wright, Thomas Percy... Thirteen of us all told. Oh, those were exciting times! Catesby! Here was a cove with an enormous vision! "What's the point of a rebellion against a king and his entire army?" says Catesby. Few enough would take up arms. A hopeless enterprise from the start and destined to fail. But, he argued, when corruption courses through the body you find the boil at the root of the infection, and drain it out. Lance the boil and save the body. Destroy this Scots pustule and the infection is spent.'

'And destroy a great many of his supporters with him. Hence the gunpowder plot to blow up the sitting Parliament.'

'Just so. But Catesby had a succession plan. Oh, yes! The grand explosion was not the end of his plans; it was yet the onset. Others of us were to kidnap the Princess Elizabeth at Coombe Abbey in Warwickshire and train her from the throne to be the Catholic monarch of England, Scotland, and Ireland as well. It was grandiose.'

'Why Princess Elizabeth? Wasn't she second in line?'

'She was but nine years old, and thus eminently biddable, yet had already graced functions at court. The eldest, Henry, would be blown to hell along with his father, but should he live, he was the spit of James; feckless gobshite. Charles and Mary were mere babes. No, Elizabeth it was.'

'In retrospect, it's astonishing that your plot almost came to fruition. There were so many ways in which it could have come adrift.'

'Oh, aye. There were spies everywhere. Walsingham's network of toads was still alive, though he was long spitted on a trident in hell. But we secured a lease on the undercroft beneath Westminster Palace without remark, and it fell to me to procure the materials and stockpile them there.'

'It's always been a wonder to me that you could acquire so many barrels of gunpowder—how many was it?—yet never be suspected.'

'Aye, I had 36 barrels of coarse mealed powder. Catesby knew a fellow in Shoreditch, name of Brock, who knew the loader of powder at the mills at Waltham Abbey. Shocking mathematician; should never have been put in charge of loading. Well, Brock would intercept the wains at Shoreditch on their way from Waltham to the armouries at Woolwich and ply the draymen with a little ale, while the mathematical discrepancy was rectified.'

'Ah, so that's how it was done. But discovery must have been on your mind continually.'

'Was discovered once. Old lady who looked after the place sees me going in, noses in to ask me what I'm doing. Well, I'm a firewood dealer and these piles of wood you see are my stock in trade. Piled to the vaulting, it was, concealing the barrels behind. Just about soiled my britches.'

'But then, you were discovered…'

'A kindness to remind me. Aye, some turncoat—I know not who—wrote a letter to Lord Monteagle telling him to, "retyre youre self into yowre contree whence yow maye expect the event in safti for… they shall receyve a terrible blowe this parliament". The writer said to burn the letter, but Monteagle took it to the king, blast his guts. We knew of the letter, but we went ahead in hopes it would be seen as a hoax. Hah! The bastard James had Sir Thomas Knyvet—long nosed, prying old file—search all the properties around Westminster Palace, and in the early hours of 5th November there was I guarding the gunpowder, practically with slow-match in hand.'

'And, of course, we all know the rest.'

'You do indeed. But I am amazed that this valiant deed of ours is still celebrated in your times.'

'There was an Act of Parliament passed in 1606, which decreed that Londoners should celebrate the King's delivery from assassination by lighting bonfires on this night, but on the proviso that "this testemonye of joy be carefull done without any danger or disorder". And so we burn a guy on the bonfire and celebrate with fireworks to this day.'

'And I'll wager the likes of old Brock made hay with it. He was ever into gunpowder and all its uses.'

'Look at this...'

'Well, I'm damned! Brock's *Guy Fawkes Mine!* I am honoured and delighted. 'Twas all worthwhile after all, wasn't it? And if I am now indeed in damnation, there's surely far worse places to be. What are you waiting for? Light those blue touchpapers!'

'And retire immediately?'

Chocolates and a True Story

I'm 93 years old and, I doubt not, only a little longer for this world.'

'It's good of you to allow me to come to Drummond Hill to visit you.'

'Aye, well, I don't know who you are or where you're from, but like all the others, I suppose you want to hear my story?'

'I certainly do, but first I've brought you a little present from the future. Here.'

'A box of chocolates! How very kind, but… but… that's *my name* on the box! Laura Secord Signature Selection? How could that be? From the future? What…?'

'Yes, indeed, it is you, and it's the continuation of a story that became a legend.'

'Continuation? Legend? You mean of things that have not yet been?'

'Absolutely. Open the box, take a chocolate.'

'I'm wandered. I'm 93 years old and sometimes there's not a lot of sense around me. These chocolates are real, though—and quite delicious; I'll have another … mmm—but I don't understand any of this. Legend?'

'Your story is now a legend.'

'My story? Things aren't clear around me—I'm 93 years old you know—but the past is crystal. They say the present goes first but the past holds true.'

'Tell me your story, please.'

'Told it often enough. I never received hardly any recognition. You know that? They didn't want to believe me. How could they? Women couldn't do what I did.'

'What *did* you do?'

'You know what I did! Let me tell it the way it was. We were Loyalists, you know, me and my husband James. Escaped America after their Revolution. We had a house in St David's with a store upstairs. When war came, James was under General Isaac Brock, God rest his soul, in the 1st Lincoln Militia. He stood by Brock and MacDonnell at Queenston

Heights in 1812 and he saw the general fall. James was injured terribly, with wounds in his leg and shoulder. I rushed to him at the camp hospital tent and they let me take him home, but when we got there… I'm sorry, even after all these years… when we got there our little home and store was looted and ruined. We stayed with Anne, our first daughter, in St David's near Queenston all that awful winter while I nursed him. He was feverish at first, then so ill he couldn't move hardly, and he lost flesh alarmingly. In May the Americans crossed the Niagara River and took Fort George, then they occupied all the land in Queenston and the Niagara region. We were surrounded now, and in enemy territory again. Any soldiers they captured they sent away, but I was nursing James so they let us stay.'

'So, they showed you some compassion.'

'Oh, in their own rough way, I suppose. He was a sergeant; I think his rank saved him. There was a company of soldiers out of Fort George billeted around us, and we accommodated a few officers and men, including Colonel Charles Boerstler. I discovered they were preparing a major offensive, even deeper into the Niagara Escarpment. That was June of 1813.'

'As far as I can tell from my reading, you never did reveal how you knew about their plans.'

'And I never have. Not even after my James passed in 1841. But I'll tell you now and make an end of it. I made friendly with one of the officers… Not so friendly as I was allowing full liberty of my person, mind you, but enough of my clothing to get into his good graces. We had trysts in the storeroom. I came right out and said I wished he could stay forever, and the fool told me he wished he could too, but the whole battalion was pushing deeper west on the morrow. I couldn't tell James. How could I? He was a jealous man, but I know now I should have… Ah, you see me now… I was so attractive then.'

'This is probably a sensitive issue, but it has seemed to

our historians to be out of character. That a wife and mother would...'

'Assumptions! Assumptions! Have things progressed no further in your age that assumptions are still made? *Women couldn't do that!* I saw an opportunity to strike at these evil people—from whom we had fled only to be enmeshed again—and I used my body to take it! I took it!'

'Please accept my apologies. So, you decided to warn your people. That was a courageous move.'

'Courageous? What would you do? I did what any decent person would. James should have gone, of course, but he could scarce move even then, and I was loath to tell him much. I had to leave him and my child in their "care", but they did treat them decent. So, I put on my cape and bonnet, stole out at night, and started to walk. The moon was in its last quarter, so it was up late and there wasn't much light. I didn't know where the British were, but I knew if I walked west, I'd get out of American territory sooner or later.'

'I have read that it was 20 miles from Queenston to the British headquarters.'

'Yes, and my feet knew it! Lieutenant FitzGibbon had his headquarters in John De Cou's house, not far from Thorold. I didn't go all that way alone, though. I came upon a camp of some Kanyen'kehà:ka warriors—Mohawks they were—who led me the rest of the way. We arrived together, and I was so footsore and totally spent that I fell unconscious on a settee in the parlour.'

'There's a famous painting of you passing on the news to FitzGibbon.'

'Tripe. I was dead to the world. The leader of the Mohawks gave them the word.'

'You can see a Mohawk warrior in the background of the painting.'

'He should have been front and centre, but I don't mind how I'm shown. I know the truth, and the word got through. That's the thing.'

'And this word made history.'

'It did indeed. Much was made of that last-moment warning.'

'The Americans were ambushed near Beaver Dams by 300 Mohawks, followed by 100 more led by Captain William Kerr. FitzGibbon finished them off with 50 men from the 49th Regiment. Colonel Boerstler surrendered.'

'Oh, I know all that. That's military history, that is! What's missing, eh?'

'Mention of Laura Secord?'

'Got it! Know what FitzGibbon wrote: "At De Cou's this morning, about seven o'clock, I received information that... the Enemy... was advancing towards me ...". Received information, he did!'

'Why would he not have mentioned you?'

'I just told you. I was asleep and doubtless nobody told him who I was, even if he knew I was there.'

'There are those in our time who wonder about the changes in your story as you have retold it over the years.'

'Show me one single person in the entire world whose story has not changed over the years and I will show you a liar! Every story changes; that's the nature of words. The fact remains that my role went quite unremarked.'

'Which is why you were obliged to petition the government for some sort of pension in recognition?'

'Yes, I petitioned in 1820 and again in 1827, and finally had FitzGibbon admit the facts. By this time, we had lost our livelihood of the store we had owned in Queenston, and James was never right again. And our daughters needed to be cared for; we were living on just James's pitiful pension and rent from a little land we owned. They turned James down flat for extra assistance, but Lieutenant-Governor Peregrine Maitland offered me the custodianship of the Brock Monument, which was to be erected to celebrate our valiant general. Throwing a bone at me, which I at first refused—I have *some* pride—and then that bastard Colbourne...'

'The Lieutenant-Governor who replaced Maitland?'

'Yes, that's the swine. Gave the keys and the stipend to someone else. Anyhow, you wanted to hear about my night-time walk through enemy territory, not some miserable tale of poverty.'

'But you did get an accolade in 1860, from Albert Edward, the Prince of Wales.'

'Oh, yes. A memorial of the War of 1812 had been prepared and I placed my signature among the heroes. Prince Albert was visiting Chippawa where the veterans were to address him. Someone told him of my little moonlit stroll, and after he went back home, he sent me £100.00. That was the only recognition I ever got.'

'In your lifetime, true.'

'And after?'

'Well, there are the chocolates. Have another… And the legend, of course.'

'Legend! I'll have none of that! What's the benefit of a legend now to a silly old woman who's losing her mind?'

'Simply, because now you know. It's all true and the world knows it. And in what time there is left to you, you can dwell not simply upon what was, but upon what will be.'

'Oh, may God bless you for that!'

Laura Secord is a household name in Canada, and not just for her 1813 heroic exploit. The candy company that bears her name was founded in 1913 by Frank P. O'Connor of Toronto. He chose Laura Secord as his brand because she was 'an icon of courage, devotion and loyalty.' And his chocolates maintain their excellence.

Some Words with Mrs Cain

Hello there! I do pan-temporal interviews and I'm here from the far future.'

'God is so weird; it's hard to keep up. Well, what is it this time? How far away?'

'Only about 6,000 years. But your people have lived in the land of Nod much longer than that, of course.'

'Depends which story you read.'

'Well, that's just it. Before I left, I was reading Chapter 4, Verse 17 of *Genesis*, so I thought I'd like to have a chat with Cain's wife.'

'Found the right person; that's me. Mrs Nobody. The bit where it says "And Cain knew his wife; and she conceived, and bare Enoch". Didn't give a mere woman a name.'

'So, do you have a name?'

'No. Dangerous precedent. Well, maybe Mrs Fratricide? Except Eve, women don't get names until much later. It's men all the way up the chain.'

'Is Cain around at the moment?'

'No. Poor bastard's a fugitive and vagabond in the earth. He's a marked man. All he really wanted was to get into my loins, and even that was only a cheap literary device.'

'How so?'

'Check the lack of more than one woman in Eden.'

'Yes, with the Adam and Eve story, we've always wondered where the women had come from to go forth and multiply with. After all, it's only much later that there's a mention of daughters. That's why I thought to talk to you.'

'Right! Takes two to tango. But look, it's not until Chapter 5, Verse 4: "And the days of Adam after he had begotten Seth were 800 years; and he begat sons *and* daughters". So, there were some girls spawned from his loins after all that time, but still on the bargain shelf with the yellow no-name label. Be practically incest anyway, wouldn't it?'

'That was 800 years after the expulsion from the Garden, though. But it was just after the killing of Abel that "Cain went out from the presence of the LORD, and dwelt in the land of Nod, on the east of Eden". That's Chapter 4, Verse 16, just before he popped into you in the next verse.'

'Oh yeah, ephemeral is Cain's missus. Y'know, it's always been a weird thing to have two "histories" running side-by-side. Here's us Noddites, lived here virtually since humankind walked out of Africa, and then there's this Eden, which God created so he could make the do-it-yourself Adam and Eve kit, the first quote/unquote couple in the world. Never made any sense to us. Here we were working like hell to get enough irrigation to scratch out a living in this arid semi-desert, and there's God creating this occupied territory where there's lakes and fountains and lush vegetation and more fruit than you'd ever hope to eat.'

'While your people were peering in through the chain-link fence and wondering.'

'And thirsting. And hungering. Huh! A Club Eden for the privileged, that's what it was. Nudist White couples' paradise, even without the sandals. Ever had an apple? They smell spectacular.'

'And then, when Adam and Eve were expelled from the Garden, Eden was left empty.'

'Shocking waste of resources. Oh, what we could have done with that land! An oasis right on our doorstep.'

'But back to the Genesis story: it seems clear to us from the far future that the author of that first book of the Bible really didn't think his plot arc through very well.'

'Damn right. He's writing away in a frenzy—got to create the entire universe and every damned thing in it in just the month of November—then he goes: Oh, shit, I forgot the girls! Now I'm stuck between incest and Oedipus!'

'Yup. Needed an editor. Kicking himself.'

'Sure. Shouldn't have been so keen to publish. Needed an editor all right, but too arrogant to employ one. They're expensive too. They charge by the Word.'

'For an ill-defined Biblical character, you seem to know a lot about publishing.'

'You're assuming I ever existed?'

'So, you could be just me talking to myself?'

'There is that possibility.'

'Hmm. Not going there. But isn't it astonishing the number of times the Bible has been translated, reworked, updated, printed and reprinted over millennia that no editorial committee ever sat down and said: Wait a minute guys, we can't let a plot hole this big go into print. Agatha Christie would never let something like this go. But we can't blue-pen it and send it back to the authors, either. Shee-it!'

'Obviously, I, Mrs Anonymous Cain, am/was the answer. Throw in a quick "knew his wife" just once and hope no one notices. I *cannot* have a name because a name denotes identity; a name would focus attention. It's deflection. Deflection relies upon anonymity; like I said, I'm just a cheap literary device. A mere sleight of penmanship.'

'There are those away in my future who say this whole tale is a parable. It's a fable, acting as a set-up to explain original sin; disobedience, jumping on top of each other, that sort of thing. It is not meant to be taken literally, and Adam and Eve were never intended to be real people. After all, assembling the universe so quickly and in such detail is also clearly quite unbelievable, let alone the bits about putting people together from mud and ribs.'

'Sensible stance. So, why did you come seek me out then?'

'Because, believe it or not, there are other people in my time who hold that *every single word* of the Bahble is the Word of Gahd, and that *every single word* is true!'

'That would explain your reluctant editors, of course.'

'Sure would. Couldn't touch it, could they? Warts and all. Like editing any novelist who's hit the *New York Times* best sellers, the list of the Untouchables. But I felt that *if* it was all true, then you would need explaining.'

'Yes, but not to you. With these "other" people of yours you, sir, have on your hands a mental health crisis of epic proportions. There's no explaining anything to them. Your problem, not mine, thank God. But where do I stand with *you*, that's the key question? Real wife, or a mere four-letter word on a page?'

'That *really is* a knife edge...'

t out from the
e LORD, and dwelt in
Nod, on the east of Eden.
Cain knew his wife; and
nceived, and bare Enoch: and
uilded a city, and called the
e of the city, after the name of
son, Enoch.
And unto Enoch was born Irad:
Irad begat Mehujael: and Me-
el begat Methusael: and Methu-
egat Lamech.
nd Lamech took unto him two

Name?
Where's this
come from?
ED

Jesus at Starbucks

It's really good of you to sit down with me at a table in Starbucks and agree to be interviewed.'

'Yeah, it's not often the Son of God can find the time. Busy up there. I feel a bit out of place without a laptop, though.'

'It's okay, I left mine at home as well.'

'Cool. This dark roast Arabica is great.'

'I find their dark roasts a little bitter, myself.'

'Oh, I'm used to gall and wormwood, and vinegar on a sponge. Fine with me.'

'I like your appearance, by the way; the shoulder-length blond hair, pale European face, the glowing white raiment.'

'Yeah, well, I get to appear in whatever guise is most appropriate, and as we're doing North American Christian, I figured this get-up would be familiar. Sort of Rembrandt or Dürer vibe. Better than the short-assed, black-haired semitic look that I carried around when I was last down here.'

'Sure. The Christians in this part of the world wouldn't appreciate you looking like their enemy.'

'Their enemy? Who said anything about enemy?'

'Anyone who doesn't believe in you, of course.'

'What? Who said believing in *me* was part of the deal?'

'Well, not believing in *you as such*, but believing in your message. You know, peace, brotherly love, treating people with respect, that sort of thing.'

'Oh, that stuff. Yeah, Dad's big Second Experiment; me coming to earth and sorting it all out. A dozen apostles to spread the gospel, setting up a bureaucratic infrastructure. My Ministry as you appropriately call it.'

'And God's intention was to have you spread the message of eternal life if people were to believe in you?'

'Believe in my message, yeah. Not me personally. Sounds simple. Had my apostles dangling that "eternal life" carrot. Amazing what you people will fall for.'

'Good Christians, I'll have you know, believe most sincerely in the promise of eternal life. It's one of the main tenets of their faith.'

'Whoo! Think it through, man! Can you even conceive of eternity? On and on and on, beyond even the heat death of the universe? You actually *want* that, you lot? Bo-o-o-ring!'

'When you put it that way… Hmm… But, tell me, why did you choose a dozen guys to spread your message back then?'

''Cuz men did everything in those days. They ran things. Women did the laundry.'

'Nothing to do with a preference for hanging around with men?'

'Hey, watch your mouth! I was just looking for power, singlemindedness, and a leavening of ruthlessness. And that's men all the way. Dangling kit was no part of it.'

'True. Just about every psychopathic, megalomaniac despot, conqueror and all-round asshole in history has been a man.'

'What the hell are you talking about?'

'Only the entire history of the world, really. But about your Ministry; what went so terribly wrong?'

'What d'you mean "terribly wrong"?'

'Jesus Christ, where have you been!? Oh, sorry. I mean… look, your followers have murdered, raped, tortured, burnt, exiled, evicted, shunned, exterminated, transported, jailed, isolated, and force-converted anyone who might disagree with them. And all in your name.'

'In the name of Christ? In my name? Jesus!'

'Yup. Absolutely. Like I said: what went wrong?'

'Well… y'know, when you've got a whole universe to watch over, you sometimes lose sight of the little details…'

'Like two thousand years of global horror and violence?'

'Jeez, you look the other way for just a couple of millennia, and look what it gets you! Complain, complain.'

'You mean you've been asleep at the switch since your resurrection? And all this has happened in your name while you tell me you weren't even *looking?*'

'It's a big universe. Your Hubble and James Webb ought

to tell you that. Can't be everywhere. Anyhow, we couldn't do anything about it even if we wanted to.'

'What do you mean "couldn't do anything"? You made this mess.'

'*Me?* Don't blame me! It's all my dad's fault.'

'God's? How?'

'You obviously don't know the first thing about Him. First off, you have this idea that He has some sort of control over this creation of His.'

'He doesn't?'

''Course he doesn't! Look around you. Read the Book. If He did, He would've stopped Satan in the Garden in the first place, wouldn't He?'

'So, you're saying He's not omniscient or precognizant, then?'

'Well, of course He isn't! Use your common sense. How could He be when He didn't see that one coming? Serpent, apple, naked private parts…'

'So, you're saying that what happens here on earth is out of His control?'

'Our control. Can you say "Judas?" I chose the bastard, don't forget.'

'Even your divine presence was capable of error, then?'

'He made me human, remember. To err is human.'

'Seems that erring is also divine. God losing control of his creation.'

'There never *was* any control. Get that into your head. Dad likes to think He controls, but he's delusional. Look at all the sinning that went on after the Fall, before He had to call in his hitman Noah for God's big First Experiment. Drown the whole bloody lot of 'em and start again, that was His tactic. Nothing by halves, that's my dad.'

'But you'll admit it didn't work.'

'Yeah, when you look at it, Noah was a pretty bad choice. The sinning started up again almost immediately. Began with him, the dirty old man. Omniscient and precognizant, my ass! Don't know where you people got that idea.'

'So, God has no control over his creation?'

'I *told* you. Never had. Never will. He built the whole thing from scratch—give Him that, it's pure genius—but He doesn't have a clue about managing it. Bit like your Elon Musk. Really, it's out of His hands.'

'So, what's all this with worshipping you both, then? Building churches, sacrifices, pilgrimages, martyrdom, all the pomp and regalia...?'

'A bit flattering quite honestly. As for me, I was just a humble carpenter back then, who just thought people should be nice to each other. And with a gift of the gab.'

'What about all the miracles?'

'Oh, how many times did I have to tell the Apostles not to invent stuff! Creative fiction goes away back. Can't blame 'em, I guess; simple fishermen.'

'Not a single miracle?'

'Nary a one.'

'Not even the water into wine trick?"

'Hah! Only thing I've ever been able to do is convert wine into vinegar. Hardly a miracle.'

'Well, this is disappointing...'

'Look, I was just a nice guy who liked hanging around and shooting the breeze. End of story.'

'I suppose, at some level we all know if we could go back over 2,000 years, we'd find a simple carpenter with a simple message.'

'Exactly. Homespun and sandals. The rest is institutionalized bullshit. Synods, committees, conclaves... a systematic, millennia-long confabulation. They even got my name wrong. It's Yeshua.'

'So, you're saying your original message is overlaid and diluted...'

'Sure is. If they got something as simple as my name wrong, whatever else did they mess with? Never thought anybody'd set fire to somebody else just because of something

I'd said. Talk about taking the ball and running with it! Right out of my bailiwick. What *is* wrong with you people?'

'Are you telling me that the entire two millennia of Christian worship expended on appealing to your goodness and your power is wasted?'

'Sure. If God could do anything about all that stuff you people pester Him with, d'you think He wouldn't intercede? Think all the jewels and gold, the silks, incense and Latin mumbling have any effect on Him at all? Sorry, man, no can do.'

'So, all that prayer and fasting and devotion; the baptism, pilgrimages, preaching, confession, atonement, conversion. All for nothing?'

'No, not for nothing. Look, it's a balance sheet, right? Or a kind of bell curve: peace, brotherly love, treating people with respect on one side, and acting like a complete shithead on the other. Both universal values in human nature.'

'So, good on one side, bad on the other. Gothic cathedrals, Bach cantatas, the Sistine Ceiling; the Inquisition, the Crusades, the martyrdoms...'

'Exactly. Either way, it's nothing to do with me and God. Washing Our hands of all that!'

'But you're really saying that Christianity is superfluous, aren't you?'

'Talk about confusing the medium with the message! *Listen!* Be good, be nice, that's the *message,* okay? As to the *medium,* choose any religion you like out of thousands, or none at all. All of them or none of them, same *message*: be good, be nice. Jesus, you people've got it real bad. Should have popped in more often. If I'd known about the coffee, I would've. This Arabica is great stuff. Never had anything like this is Galilee.'

'Oh, shut up and drink your dark roasted gall and wormwood.'

One-on-One with God

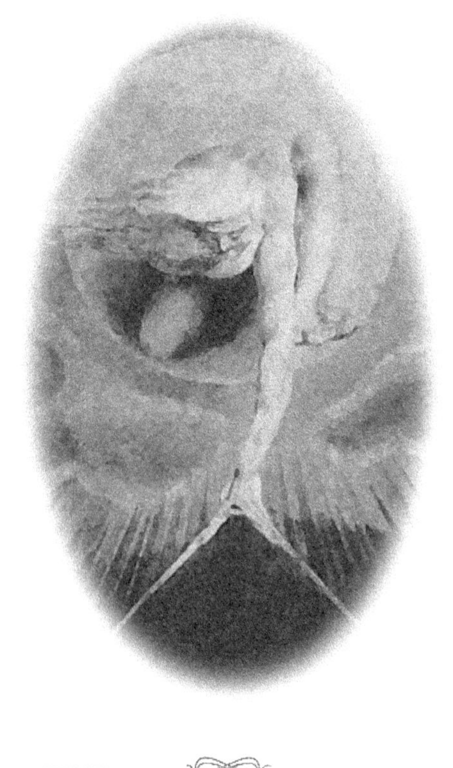

Now, look here, I'm really busy, so what do you want? And make it quick!'

'I believe this is the first time you've ever met with anybody one-on-one.'

'What do you mean one-on-one? I do it all the time.'

'Yes, but those people who claim to speak for you are proxies. They relay what they think you said. You always speak to the world through intermediaries, who then write it all down in holy books or hold forth from a pulpit.'

'And you're different how?'

'Well, I'm sitting down with you in my office right now, whereas with your chosen prophets you simply put thoughts into their heads. You lurk in people's brains; you're a predator on the mentally ill.'

'Oh, am I? So, unlike every other prophet, seer, mystic, shaman, Bible Belt evangelist, juju-man, and mushroom junkie in the history of humankind, you alone think I'm sitting here in your office on this five-wheeled swivel chair from Staples, just waiting to be interrogated? Is that it?'

'Well, yes...'

'Off your lithium today, are you?'

'No, no. I'm as sane as the next man. You obviously exist.'

'Well, judging by the preceding 24 interviews, I think your sanity is definitely a matter of debate. And, as a corollary, so is my existence.'

'I'll have you know I was an existentialist before you sat down in that chair. Your presence has converted me.'

'Well great, because I get really pissed with people throwing Kierkegaard and Nietzsche at me. And when they toss in Sartre along with the nihilists, I feel like smiting them.'

'So, you should be happy that I've called you here, that you are tangibly real, and that they've been proven wrong.'

'Whatever! Now you know the answer, don't you? Look, I've got a whole bloody universe to run and you're wasting precious time with silliness.'

'Not silly at all. The entire history of mankind hinges on the very question of your existence. And here you are!'

'Good. I exist. And you know damned well if I didn't exist, your lot would have invented me anyway. End of story. Now can I get back to building these galaxies, *please?*'

Bonus Track

'I've been waiting for over half an hour. Another six-ounce Pinot Noir please.'

'Here you go. So, you decided to interview this guy in a wine bar?'

'That was the idea.'

'Founder of a major religion, you say?'

'Yup.'

'Lucky for you he's not gonna show.'

'Lucky? How come?'

'You inviting a fatwa, or what?'

'Yeah, that was kinda stupid, wasn't it?'

'Dodged a bullet.'

'Sure did. Cheers!'

Coda

Well, there they are: the *really* true stories of 25 of our favourite characters from myth, history, folklore and legend, most obligingly related to a very receptive and somewhat informed interviewer. We live in an era when truth is a commodity that can be bought, sold, and repackaged in many forms. Characters from the past—real, fictional, or somewhere in between—are merely the raw material on the shop floor, and it is up to us how the finished merchandise is created and retailed.

My brand should be on supermarket shelves everywhere.

www.ingramcontent.com/pod-product-compliance
Lightning Source LLC
Chambersburg PA
CBHW030503100426
42813CB00002B/315

* 9 7 8 1 9 8 8 6 5 7 3 8 7 *